WHEN THE COUNTRY WAS NEW

by

Jeannette (Jenny) Entsminger

IN LOVING MEMORY
OF MY GRANDMOTHER
JEANNETTE CECELIA CULLISON
(June 18, 1900 to December 24, 1992)

He hath shewed thee, O man, what is good; and what doth the Lord require of thee, but to do justly, and to love mercy, and to walk humbly with thy God? Micah 6:8 (KJV)

PREFACE

This book includes time treasured memories lovingly passed down to me by my grandmother, Jeannette Cullison, for whom I was named. These stories tell of my grandmother's extraordinary childhood in Garfield County, Oklahoma. Her parents, James and Mary Cullison, settled in Garfield County just outside of Enid, Oklahoma as part of the 1893 land rush. My grandmother was born in 1900, and the events described in this book took place between 1893 to 1917. As a young girl, I recall listening to my grandmother sharing her most adventurous childhood memories. These stories provoked awe in me at the challenges that my courageous ancestors faced in settling this new land. My grandmother fondly referred to this era as "When the Country was New."

To preserve the authenticity of her memories, the stories in this book are shared through the first-person voice of my grandmother as a young girl. Some expressions and descriptions may not be politically correct by today standards but are shared as passed down for sake of accuracy. The appendix includes some original family writings and poems as well as photos from the era. It is my great joy to pass on these family treasures to a new generation of Oklahomans who live more than 100 years later.

I also especially wish to dedicate this book to my beautiful and wonderful mother, Jeanneane Hall, who passed away last year. It was her greatest desire to see these stories from her mother passed down. I know she would be incredibly pleased that this book has become a reality.

Jenny Entsminger

3

INTRODUCTION

The Cullison Family History

James Buchanon Cullison was born on September 21, 1857 in New London, Iowa to Elisha and Matilda Macabe Cullison. He was the father of my grandmother, Jeannette Cullison. He served as a judge for many years in Enid Oklahoma and was eventually elected to the Oklahoma Supreme Court.

When Judge Cullison was a child, his pioneer parents moved to Adair County, Missouri where they purchased an 800-acre plantation. The plantation house was large with seven fireplaces. Judge Cullison's father was a Democrat and a slave owner. However, over time, he came to greatly admire Abraham Lincoln, pledged his loyalty to the Union, and voluntarily freed his slaves.

James Cullison was the tenth of twelve children and was orphaned at the age of fifteen. He attended Valparaiso College in Indiana and the Eastern Iowa Normal School. While attending college, he met Mary May Sharp. Mary was the oldest child of Cecelia Jeannette Greenman and Alonzo White Sharp of New York. On July 30, 1882, James and Mary married in Wayne, Iowa. James taught school in Kirksville, Iowa for several years.

In 1885, driven by the fervor to find a new place to live, James and Mary moved along with their infant, Jimmy, to the wild Kansas prairie. This marked the birth of the small town of Cullison in Pratt County, Kansas. Later, Mary proudly shared with her daughter, Jeannette, about setting the family's rustic table with a fine linen cloth each evening even though their initial home was a primitive dugout without running water or electricity.

The Cullison family soon moved again 150 miles west to Hugoton, Kansas. This settlement was first named Hugo in honor of French writer Victor Hugo, but soon changed its name to Hugoton to distinguish it from Hugo, Colorado. In Hugoton, James practiced law, served as the deputy superintendent of public instruction and was appointed as the clerk of the district court. There were only two other women who lived in the county. Mary Cullison, in her kindness, baked dozens of loaves of homemade bread for all the homesick young men.

Within a few years, crops failed due to drought, the earth hardened, and declining agricultural prices brought panic among the settlers. The Cherokee Indians in the Oklahoma territory agreed to sell large areas of land to the federal government. These events led to the Oklahoma land runs of 1889 and 1893. The 1889 land run was the first land run, and the 1893 land run was the largest.

On September 16, 1893, James Cullison, his pregnant wife Mary, and their three children, including a toddler, joined about one hundred thousand anxious pioneers to stake their claim to land that had formerly been Cherokee grazing property. It is that historical event that begins the story told below. The property upon which the Cullison family settled was a farm approximately six miles east of what became Enid, Oklahoma.

In 1897, President McKinley appointed James Cullison the register of the United States Land Office in Enid in which role he served for five years. After Oklahoma became a state on November 16, 1907, James B.

Cullison became the first Judge of Garfield County and then District Judge in 1911. James B. Cullison later served as a Justice of the Supreme Court of Oklahoma from 1929-1831. In 1936, James B. Cullison died at the age of 79 in Enid, Oklahoma. Mary died in 1948.

James and Mary faced many challenges on the new frontier. They showed great courage and fortitude in settling a new land. They were pillars of integrity and stamped their mark for good in Oklahoma's history. Together James and Mary had seven children – three boys and four girls. My grandmother, Jeannette Cecelia Cullison was their youngest child. Jeannette was bold, outgoing, and possessed a keen sense of humor. Although her mother was aghast at birthing a seventh child at a late age, Jeannette cared for her mother into her elderly years forming an inseparable bond.

Jeannette's six older siblings, who are prominently described in the stories below, are listed as follows:

> *James Buchanon Cullison, Jr.* was known as "Jimmy." He was gentle, serious, and an exemplary role model for his younger siblings. His appearance resembled his father with dark hair, fair complexion and freckles. He became an attorney and married Laura Searcy of Gerber Oklahoma,

> *Tyra Cullison* was the second child of James and Mary and died of whooping cough at the age of two years. Mary grieved his loss for the rest of her life.

June Beatrice Cullison was the eldest daughter. She was prim and proper with long dark hair and a pale complexion. Her Irish temperament fueled her dramatic persona. She attended Mount Carmel Girls School in Wichita, Kansas and later published a book about Indian tribes of Oklahoma. June stole the hearts of many suitors and eventually married William J. Otjen, a soldier in the Spanish-American war. June and her husband had four children. As tragically described in the story below, their first child, Mary Catherine, perished of a heart condition at the age of two.

Irene Margaret Cullison was the fourth child. Described as tall, whimsical and intelligent, she projected a charm that endeared herself to others. She was Jeannette's favorite sister. As a teacher she obtained a master's degree in Psychology and served as one of the founding educators of the Montessori Academy. She was employed by the creators of "Chautauqua," a travelling assembly of speakers, musicians and showmen that strived to bring culture to communities across the nation. Irene married William Vaught of Washington, D.C. Irene's life was filled with tragedy, including the untimely death of her husband and suicide of her seventeen-year-old son. Yet, when asked to reflect on her life, she would readily reply, "I have had a wonderful life."

Mary Elisabeth Cullison was the fifth child and known as "May." May was a gifted piano player. She also became a teacher in Wichita, Kansas. May married John Myers, a ranchman from Dover, Oklahoma.

Douglas Lincoln Cullison was the sixth child and greatly adored by my grandmother. His brilliant inquisitives led him into mischief. Later in life, he travelled around the world. My grandmother often said, "He was misunderstood by his teachers." Douglas married Beatrice Walker of New York.

Chapter One - The New Frontier

It was September 16, 1893. Mary Cullison threw the last blanket into the covered wagon. Weeks of packing and planning had come to an end. Her toddler, Irene, clung to her skirt, hot and dusty, and whimpering softly. The older children, Jimmy and June, stood restless next to the wagon. Mary's belly was swollen with child. Her arms ached to hold Tyra, her son who had been lost to whooping cough several winters before. With her hair pulled tightly in a bun and her frayed bonnet bleached from the sun, she stretched her aching back and looked across the line into a land unknown. Unlike her more docile cousins in New York, Mary exhibited a pioneer spirit of patience, endurance, and strength. She was determined to make a new life in this Oklahoma Territory.

Seeking a new country with determined hearts and hopeful spirits, thousands came. Boomer camps with tents and other makeshift dwellings popped up all along the southern Kansas border. Everywhere around were reminders of the drought -- parched fields and the blistering sun.

James Cullison, whose family would later refer fondly as "the Judge," was apprehensive but inwardly desperate to make the run. Sweat dripped from his brow, and his thick hair ruffled in the wind. He hurled the children into the wagon like sacks of grain. Mary and the children remained in the wagon as James Cullison proceeded on his horse to the line. The clanking wagon wheels turned around and around. The rocking of the wagon cradled the children to sleep.

The land run began exactly at noon. It was the largest of the Oklahoma land runs. More than 115,000 people registered and as many as 150,000 participated. There were 42,000 parcels of land to be claimed. When the gun sounded, a mad rush of horses, wagons and even bicycles raced across the border. James Cullison assumed a brisk pace on his horse for about 50 miles until he came to a tract of land in the county designated simply by the letter "O." This tract was six miles east of the town of Enid in what would soon become Garfield County. James Cullison put down his "stake" to make his claim.

After unhitching his exhausted horse, James went in search of water. Over a grassy knoll, he saw two men sitting next to a campfire leisurely cooking a meal. Seeing they had been settled for some time and knowing the pace he had kept, James was certain they had come before the legal time of entry. They were "Sooners." However, to avoid a dispute, James Cullison paid them $300 that they demanded to relinquish their claim.

Soon after staking this claim, James Cullison returned and brought his family to their new home. In the fall of 1893, James and Mary Cullison moved their family to "Quality Hill" in east Enid. A daughter, May, was the first of the Cullisons born in Oklahoma. James Cullison practiced law and was elected the first Justice of Peace in Patterson Township in Garfield County. In 1897, he was appointed by President McKinley as Registrar of the United States Land Office. He served in that position for five years and decided more than 6,000 land contests.

It was the autumn of 1899. Mary Cullison was 40 years old, settled in the new territory, and immersed in building the township of Enid. She had five living children: Jimmy, June, Irene, May, and Douglas. Their second child, Tyra, had died an infant. May and Douglas had been born after the family settled in Enid. May was the first baby ever born in Enid.

Originally called Skeleton, the town's name was changed to Enid after a character in Alfred Lord Tennyson's *Idylls of the King*. However, a more colorful tale grew up over the years about the origin of the town's name. According to that tale, some early settlers set up a chuckwagon and hung a sign that read "DINE". Supposedly some other more free-spirited settlers turned the sign backward to read "ENID".

The Cullison house was on Grand Street six blocks from the City Square. Judge Cullison had added several rooms since acquiring the property and building the house. The house was constructed of white clapboard trimmed in green. The two front doors had frosted glass panes etched in a deer and hunting scene. The front lawn was planted with Bermuda grass. An 80-acre farm extended behind the house which included a barn, pastureland, and areas planted with wheat, corn and vegetables.

Mary knew it was true - the nausea and the increasing headaches - she had experienced this feeling too often before. With child again, and at her age, it was shameful! She was greatly disturbed about her condition. The Judge just chuckled when he heard the news. Mary seldom spoke harshly to her husband, but her dark emotions surged, "You wouldn't be laughing if someone was going to chop off your leg." Turning, she stormed out of her bedroom onto the side porch. The cool October wind grazed her hair. She sat softly on the swing, soulfully confirming this would be her last child. In a moment, the Judge came out, taking her hand, he sat down beside her and stroked her hair. "I love you," he said, "And I love you," she replied.

When the baby came months later, so did the repetitious agony of labor. This time lacked the joy and wonder of her first childbirth. Pain seized her in fatigue and mocked her age and frailties. She because dizzy and weak, seemingly drifting from the bonds of life that tethered her soul to the earth. Fervently, she prayed for her life and for the life of her child. Finally, after hours of labor, she brought forth a small raven-haired girl. She named her Jeannette Cecelia Cullison after her own beloved mother.

June was furious! Her mother had given birth to a new baby. She couldn't begin to comprehend why. As a self-absorbed adolescent, June construed this intrusion as a personal attack. In retaliation, she refused to help. Her mother lay in bed, weak and exhausted with the baby swaddled next to her. It was difficult for Mary to pick up the baby and nurse. She needed June's help. At least Irene and May were there to support her.

In a fit of self-pity, June burst into her mother's room. The dress she wanted to wear to school the next day had not been ironed. "Mother! My dress is all wrinkled and I cannot wear it like this!" "Honey", Mary answered gently, "I cannot get out of bed, I am far too weak. You will have to iron it yourself." With that, June tossed the dress onto the bed and ran from the room. She hurried to the barn with angry tears burning her eyes. She sat in the haystack and brooded all day.

"How disgusting," June thought over and over. It was embarrassing – having a baby at her mother's age. The barn door creaked open, and June peered from behind the haystack. Her father's stern face appeared with nostrils flaring in anger. His voice quivered a low tone.

June blurted, "I don't know why she had to have that stupid ole' baby anyway?" Silence was followed by heavy breathing. She knew she had pushed her dear Papa to the edge, and she waited for his wrath. He spoke, "June, you are spoiled and insolent. I'm ashamed and disgraced by your behavior. Go right now and apologize to your mother. and for God's sake. June, help her. I feel very sorry for you if you don't."

June moved slowly past her father and reluctantly headed for her mother's bedroom. Her father's words of discipline had penetrated her selfishness. June was ashamed and now afraid. It wasn't the apology she dreaded so much as the speech her mother would likely deliver afterwards – a speech she knew she fully deserved. She entered the room, and her mother was sleeping. June caught a glimpse of the "impish" creature lying in the crib. She saw a tiny baby lay sucking her thumb. June's heart melted. A baby! She was prettier than her own china doll. June suddenly realized that it could be like her baby too. It didn't have to be all Mama's.

June picked up the baby and sat down next to Mama. As her mother stirred, June said "She's beautiful Mama, I'm sorry I was such a ninny!" June then asked, "What will you name her -- Jeannette Cecelia Cullison

13

after grandmother?" Her mother replied, "Yes, only we will call her Janey." June crooned, "Little Janey - little precious baby, rock-a-bye." June reached to hug her mother and deeply apologized again.

Chapter Three - Grandma's Visit

It was the summer of 1908. I was the youngest of the Cullison children, and my family called me "Janey." I had just turned 8 years old. Oklahoma was a brand-new state having been admitted to the Union in 1907. Enid was growing quickly. The 80-acre farm behind our house had been transformed into the Cullison Addition with many new homes. My father had built many of these homes with his own hands. They were simple homes, all with large front porches. Papa, in thoughtfulness, had planted trees around each house.

My sister June filled her days designing party dresses for the dances she would attend during her last year at Mt. Carmel Girl's School in Wichita Kansas. They were all lovely, but one fascinated me. This dress was a floor length gown with a small glittering butterfly on the bodice. To June's delight, my mother would diligently work for hours sewing these dresses. June would also sew some, doing the handwork or tatting a lace collar to make the garment even lovelier.

With my mother and June devoted to domestic projects, I sneaked off to the square to meet my best friend, Betsy Drummond, for hopscotch. The square was teaming with people as it served as the center of our community. The county courthouse stood upon the square surrounded by a large green lawn with park benches at either end. Young trees were growing all around the square. My father, with Jimmy's help, had taken great pleasure in planting each one. The first tree planted was an elm tree located at the southwest corner which my father had removed as a sapling from "Skeleton Ford." This tree is now known as the "Judge Cullison

Elm." For several months after planting the trees, Papa diligently carried water from the creek to the park until the trees began to flourish.

In the business of the day, people paused to chat and catch up on local news and gossip. Betsy and I turned away from our hopscotch to listen, and our ears grew larger as they talked. Today, we overheard about the postman's two daughters who were taken by dysentery from eating too many over ripe cherries. The medicines had failed, and they continued to decline. I was alarmed and decided I would only eat ten cherries a day, and only then if I was tempted to eat any at all.

Betsy and I walked from the square and passed by Mr. Godschalk's clothing store. We admired the fine men's suits displayed in the window. Mr. Godschalk took great pride in the quality of the clothes he sold, and he ordered most of his merchandise and materials from New York. We were aware that Mr. Godschalk was expecting his betrothed to arrive from Holland any day. They would be married under a canopy as was the custom of Jews. Mr. Godschalk had not seen or spoken to his fiance' for five years. She did not know a word of English, and I wondered how she would acclimate coming from such a distant land. I prayed she would be happy as we all loved dear Mr. Godschalk and his wonderful store of men's finery. Satisfied we had seen all we needed to see, Betsy and I walked home from our adventures in town.

Just past twilight, I laid outside on a soft blanket underneath the cottonwood. My mother came and told me someone special was coming to visit. I couldn't imagine who. "It's Grandma Sharp," she shared, "All the way from Iowa." I squealed in delight. I adored my Grandma Sharp, and her visits were rare. I would sneak up and sleep with her in the big feather bed in the attic, and we would giggle in the dark. Grandma Sharp always had a special fondness for me - maybe because I was the youngest and her namesake. Turning back to Mother, I shouted, "Fantastic!" My mother was pleased and amused by my enthusiastic response.

Mama and I looked up to the sky in the still summer night. She pointed out the big and little dipper. I sat in her lap, and she held me close. Mama spoke softly as the stars shimmered above, "You're going to have to help her, Janey. She is not as young as she used to be and I'm afraid the long journey may exhaust her." Then Mama chuckled under her breath as she recalled Grandma Sharp referring to the Oklahoma Territory as "the falling off place." Mama explained to me this meant the end of the world. "I'll do my best, Mama," I assured her as we returned to the house and climbed wearily up the stairs. I fell gratefully into bed.

Grandma Sharp was a brilliant woman who could recite long stanzas from Burns, Wordsworth and other poets. She learned all of these poems before she was 10 years old just as my mother did. Now I was learning them too. Grandma was also a gifted musician with a trained singing voice and the rare ability to play the melodeon, a small German accordion.

The knots in my rag curls pressed tight into the back of my neck, and I was awakened by the horses' "clickity-clack, clickity-clack." It was old Nellie pulling the carriage. That meant Grandma was here. I flew down the stairs hearing her jolly loud chuckle echo throughout the house. I wrapped my arms around her enormous frame. She slowly bent down and asked, "How is my little one?" I replied, "Oh, fine, Grandma, just great. I'm so pleased you are here!"

The whole family was caught up hugging Grandma and exchanging greetings. To get her attention, I blurted, "Grandma, I like your dress." She looked bewildered and replied, "I look like a mess?" Horrified but amused that she had misinterpreted me, I yelled loudly, "Grandma, I like your dress!" She smiled and patted my head, "Thank you, sweetie."

Time passed too quickly when Grandma came to visit. There were never enough hours in the day to do all the things I wanted to do with her. We took Grandma to town, pointing out each building and home. Shopping was so much fun! Grandma bought me candy at the general store.

When we came home that afternoon, Mama climbed down the cellar ladder and brought up brightly colored jars of peaches. Mama's homemade peach cobbler was a bit of heaven and that was the dessert she was preparing for dinner. As Papa said grace at the outset of dinner, I anxiously waited to sink my teeth into the delicious cobbler.

After the cobbler was devoured by all and dinner dishes cleared, the family gathered in the parlor. The parlor was carpeted in a Persian design velvet carpet. Nearly every evening, Mama or May played the piano, and we all sang along. June sang in her sweet soprano voice. Significant musical talents had been passed down from generation to generation in our family. Like her mother, Mama was an accomplished meledeon and organ player. Her father, Alonzo Sharp, and grandfather, Salmon, played the violin. They had organized popular music schools in their communities back East. Some had been conducted in their home and others in the country schoolhouse.

My father possessed an avid love for hymns. The Judge especially loved the songs written by Stephen Foster. On this occasion, everyone joined in - except for me. I had to wash the dishes. Being the youngest had its drawbacks. I worried this evening that by the time I could play and sing, everyone would be tired of listening. The dishes were finally sparkling clean, and I went into the parlor to join the family.

When the concert concluded, we clambered up the stairs and changed into our nighties. After everyone else was asleep, I tip-toed to the attic to be with Grandma. As the door creaked open, Grandma whispered, "Come on in, Janey." I snuggled next to her and listened attentively as she shared about all the military heroes in our family. She recounted the Civil War adventures of her father, Alonzo Sharp, a New York State Senator who had fought for the Union. She told me about her grandfather, Salmon Sharp, of Washington, Connecticut, who fought in the war of 1812. There was also her great-grandfather, Eliakim Sharp of Locke, New York, who had served under Captain Ichabod Turner during the Revolutionary War. My eyelids eventually grew heavy with sleep.

The next morning, I brought Grandma breakfast on a tray and helped her find her shoes. She was so fat that she had a terrible time bending down to tie her shoes. I tied them for her. Recognizing my grandma's helplessness, I suggested, "What you need Grandma is a maid." Her reply was, "An egg? I couldn't eat one if I had one." I laughed out loud. Confused, she asked what was so humorous. Talking as loud as

I could without shouting, I told her I had asked if she needed a maid - not an egg. She roared and cackled at herself. Finally, we stopped giggling and gave each other a big hug.

The weeks passed quickly. Grandma would be leaving today, and I knew I would miss her with all my heart. I watched as Mama began to swallow hard and her eyes filled with tears as she waved good-bye to her mother. It was hard for me to imagine not seeing my mother every single day. I hoped that part of growing up would never come to pass.

Chapter Four - English Lessons

Summer passed and autumn would soon erupt into a brightly colored countryside. Jimmy was returning today to school in Missouri. His copper hair tousling in the wind, his dignified military school uniform, and his quiet gentle demeanor were the mental images I held of him through the years.

June was also ready to head back to school. She looked elegant in her new traveling dress. The entire household had catered to her all summer. Only yesterday, she strutted into the house puffed up in her dark blue velvet riding habit with matching hat and plume. Reviewing her monthly allowance, she dramatically threw her hand to her forehead and sobbed, "Poverty, nothing but poverty." I knew that our family was well off compared to many. My mother had employed a colored lady, Mrs. O'Banyion, to do the wash. That was a luxury not many in Enid had those days. But June saw things differently, and now she was off to Mt. Carmel, with party dress and all. I prayed she'd have a glorious final year. I would miss her eventually, I supposed.

The day after Jimmy and June left for school, Mama and I went to Mr. Godschalk men's clothing store to find a gift to buy for the Judge's soon approaching birthday. We observed that Mrs. Godschalk was with child. She seemed sad and helpless, still unable to speak a word of English. Mr. Godschalk appeared from the back room with downcast eyes. My mother was filled with compassion for this young couple. Mama asked if Mrs. Godschalk would enjoy making baby clothes and invited her to our house for tea the following day. Mr. Godschalk 's face lit up in joy, "God bless you! Maybe this will lift her spirits."

Mrs. Godschalk arrived at our door in a beautiful lace shirt and long blue linen skirt. She looked eloquent. Her hair was gathered in a knot arrayed with a beautiful pearl comb. She was an attractive lady with dark auburn hair and crystal blue eyes. She was delighted to be in our home. She brought Mama a gift - a dainty linen handkerchief with pastel colors woven in fine threads. We had never seen anything like it. It came from Holland. I thought to myself that Holland must be filled with magnificent treasures.

Then Mrs. Godschalk opened a wooden box. Inside were miniature bolts of fine fabric also from her native land. This was the material she planned to use to sew her baby items. Mother smiled as she carefully placed each bolt upon the table stating slowly and clearly, "Material." Mrs. Godschalk would repeat, "Material." Then, mother would say, "Needle and thread." Mrs. Godschalk would repeat the words and giggle. This process continued with Mama pointing out many different items in the room. Mrs. Godschalk would listen carefully and slowly repeat back the English word for each item. With each new word learned, my mother nodded in approval. She assured Mrs. Godschalk that she was learning to speak English well.

I was delighted to serve them tea and corn muffins as the lesson continued. It was the first of many afternoons that Mrs. Godschalk spent with my mother preparing the layette for the baby and learning to speak English. Soon Mrs. Godschalk was able to understand simple conversations. She appreciated my mother. Each time she left our house, she turned to my mother and proudly enunciated in perfect English, "Thank you Mrs. Cullison." She also continued to bring us pots of her delicious matzo ball soup.

Chapter Five - The Circus Trick

It was early October and the weather in Enid was still mild. Saturdays were especially fun days. I couldn't believe the contraption my sisters, May and Irene, had rigged up in the barn. They were adventurous teenagers, and I was a willing follower. The idea came from a circus picture book that my father had in his library.

The barn was about 150 feet behind the house and surrounded by honey locust trees. Our carriage and horse Nellie were kept there. May and Irene had constructed two swings with wooden bars that hung about nine feet above the barn floor. There were piles of fluffy golden hay underneath. May and I would climb up one side of the barn, and Irene would climb up the other. As May mounted her swing, she maneuvered my legs over the bar on which she was seated. Then, with May seated and me hanging upside down, she would let go, and we would fly. Irene would take off at precisely the same moment. Somewhere in mid-air, Irene grabbed my hands and my legs slid off May's bar flipping me right side up. Swinging fast to the other side of the barn, Irene would drop me into the hay before I crashed into the barn wall. I bounced softly in the hay squealing in excitement.

Believing that we were safe entertaining ourselves and that the older girls would protect their little sister, Mother never worried about what took place in the barn. We had practiced our circus stunt several times, and we were growing tired. However, we decided to try it one more time - striving for perfection. The final feat was almost complete when Irene, distracted, failed to let go of my hands. Seeing I was about to crash into the barn wall, I closed my eyes, clinched my teeth, and awaited the sickening thud. BOOM.

Upon impact, the wind was knocked out of me. As I caught my breath, a stinging sensation shot up my nose and blood poured into my eyes. I could not see, but I felt a warm stickiness pouring out all over my face. Irene and May screamed. In a frenzy, they ran in all directions at once. With the screaming and commotion, I was terrified for a moment that I might lose my life. Irene ran for Mama, and May ran for Dr. Fields. I was left bleeding alone in the hay.

My mother sprang into the barn with a first aid kit in hand. She wiped the blood from my eyes and observed a small tear on my nose. A hook protruding from the barn wall had caught my nostril and torn it. The doctor soon arrived. Examining me closely, Dr. Fields announced, "Janey will be ok, but she will need a few stitches." My mother was shaken - half angry at our mischief and half relieved I wasn't seriously hurt. She snapped, "Mercy, Jeannette, your face is going to look like a map of Europe."

Mama pursed her lips and squeezed my hand as Dr. Fields applied the stitches. I felt a terrible stinging sensation and moaned as the doctor tediously completed his task. Mama took me inside, changed my blood-soaked clothes, and accompanied me to my bed. I was exhausted by the trauma. She cautiously kissed my forehead and reminded me how fortunate I had been. "It could have been your eye," she said.

I awoke the following day and my nose was swollen and throbbing – a stark reminder of our folly the day before. Mama summoned Irene,

May and me into the drawing room and shut the door behind her. She turned and said, "I thought about what kind of punishment I should administer so this calamity will not be repeated. I decided not to punish you corporally as your sister's nose is a reminder of your foolishness." Instead, Mama told us that she was going to tell us a true story that should never pass beyond our doors. She explained, "This is a story about how catastrophes can alter one's life. Jeannette was more fortunate than Mr. Johnston, I believe."

Chapter Six - A Missed Love

Mr. Johnston owned the grain store downtown. It was a substantial business especially for Enid. Mr. Johnston was a kind man who limped badly. Each year, before winter set in, he gave barrels of grain to the poor and to the colored people who lived in "the hollow." He had a son, Glen Johnston, who wasn't so kind. Glen was always dipping my pigtails in his inkwell. What a bully!

Our focus was now fully on Mama as she began her story about catastrophes and their consequences. She told us that when Mr. Johnston had been 3 years old, he had toddled in on a newly mopped floor. When he slipped, his mother tried but failed to catch him. Upon impact with the floor, he broke his leg. The doctor was called but set the leg incorrectly. The bone grew back in a twisted manner causing Mr. Johnston to be disabled just as he remains today.

Mr. Johnston learned as a young man to cope with his adversity. For most people, his warm and friendly personality compensated for his withered leg - except for the young woman with whom he had fallen madly in love. She was the beautiful daughter of a prominent Enid lawyer. Mr. Johnston requested her hand in marriage, but she flatly denied him because of his twisted leg. She cruelly told him that she couldn't marry a "cripple."

Before this rejection, Mr. Johnston had almost forgotten his childhood misfortune. Now, crushed and broken hearted, it defeated him. For years, he did not smile or laugh. He wore a sullen and vacant stare upon his face and avoided social gatherings. Then he met Ollie, married and had a family. He had two sons, Dale and Glen, and a daughter named Mary Ester. Life became much better, but Mr. Johnston never forgot the pain of losing his first love.

My mother then explained the moral of this story. If a physical mutilation of your face or body would occur because of childhood silliness or folly, you would bear the burden the rest of your life. It would be a constant battle fought inwardly diminishing your self-worth. You would always be worried how others perceived you. Though people may seem charitable in their own way, they might reject you just as that young woman did for Mr. Johnston. Remember girls, "God just gives you one body, it is yours to keep healthy and whole. It is the temple of the Holy Spirit. Please cherish your bodies and protect them as I have nurtured them from infancy and desire no permanent scars upon them."

A heaviness gripped our spirits, and we felt sorry for Mr. Johnston. I was grateful that I would not be mutilated for life. But I would always wear the small scar from this injury as a reminder of our silly childish stunt. We knew our mother had forgiven us. We grabbed her hand and promised we would be careful from now on.

In a few more days June was coming home from Mt. Carmel for a long weekend. Her new beau, Mr. Otjen, would be calling. He was a soldier who fought in the Spanish-American War. He presented so dashing and handsome. I hoped June appreciated him. If she didn't, I thought I would surely tell her she should.

Chapter Seven - An Unjust Punishment

I was 10 years old. My father had just been elected as District Judge of Garfield County, a position to which he would be reelected 5 more times. I attended the same elementary school as my brother Douglas. My devotion to Douglas was intense.

One day, as I was standing in the square, I looked up at my father's office window and caught the eye of Douglas. He was visiting the Judge. I smiled and waved energetically, and he grinned and waved back. Later that night, he told me that, at first glance, he thought I was a beautiful little Indian girl playing in the courtyard. "Douglas, you are so silly!" I exclaimed. But I cherished the word "beautiful" that he had used in describing me. June attracted all the suitors. May and Irene were turning into pretty young women. But at least Douglas, in a moment unaware, had shown me at ten years old that I had potential to be beautiful too.

Douglas had a reputation among his teachers as being a smart aleck. Douglas was brilliantly versed on a multitude of topics, and his knowledge on many subjects exceeded that of his teachers. That greatly annoyed them. One teacher had it in for Douglas. If he answered a question and added any more information than required, she would jerk him to his feet, grab his ear and pull him into the "whipping room." The school was built on a slight hill. Outside the whipping room there was a pile of cinders so high, you could stand on top of it and peer into the window. The older children would stand on the cinder pile and strain their necks to view Douglas receiving his licks. His punishment was administered in an excessive and cruel way.

The teacher forced Douglas to remove his shirt and lashed his back several times with a rawhide whip. The rawhide cut into his flesh and drew blood, leaving large purple welts. Douglas never cried out even though these beatings were extremely painful.

Standing on the cinder pile, I viewed this terrible punishment only once. It was all I could take to see my beloved Douglas tortured in this inhumane way. Though he did not cry out, I saw tears in forming in the corners of his eyes. When he glanced toward the window and our eyes met, I felt ashamed for watching. I was horrified and tears soon began streaming down my cheeks in compassion.

I turned and ran like the wind to fetch Papa. My heart was beating fast, and I gained speed as I approached the courthouse. Surely Papa would rescue Douglas from his tormentor. Bursting into Papa's office, my emotions overtook me. My body shook with great sobs, "Papa, Papa, they are beating Douglas with a rawhide whip at school."

My father was instantly unsettled by this news. He put his pen down, grabbed his coat and derby hat, and strutted toward the school. His gait was quick, and his expression angry. I followed closely behind. When we reached the school, Papa headed directly for the "whipping room." He threw open the door without knocking. Upon entering, we quickly noticed the room was empty. However, lying across a chair was the rawhide whip that the monster teacher had used. There were blood stains on the tip of it. Papa picked up the whip and ran his hands across the leather. Contempt and anger seethed from Papa's soul as he contemplated the cruel and unnecessary punishment that had been inflicted upon his son.

One of Douglas' schoolmates told Papa and me that Douglas had been sent home. We quickly left for our house. Mama had taken Douglas' shirt off and was tenderly washing his back with soap and water. The welts were still fresh. In great pain, Douglas worried about what Papa might do when he found out he had been punished again at school. This time, Papa's eyes filled with compassion as he placed his hand on Douglas' shoulder and stated, "This will never happen again, son."

That night I heard Douglas writhing in pain as the welts on his back throbbed. His moans echoed through the house and weighed heavy on our hearts. The following week, Douglas enrolled at St. Joseph's Institute, a Catholic school staffed by six nuns who had come from San Antonio, Texas. The cruelty of the prior school was behind him. It was a new start for Douglas. I was confident that his brilliance would now have the opportunity to shine as a thousand stars in the sky.

Chapter Eight - *Where There's Smoke There's Fire*

School on this mild October day had been boring, and I was feeling mischievous as I walked home by myself. I spied a match that had hidden itself under a leaf on the sidewalk. In curiosity, I reached down and struck it on a brick. The second time I struck the match, a yellow spark flew but seemed to instantly die. Fire was so mesmerizing. I knew it was dangerous, and I quickly glanced both ways to see if anyone had witnessed my senselessness.

Suddenly, I heard an old lady running toward me, screaming and shaking her fists. Her eyes were crazed, and her grey hair was frazzled. This was the old witch of the neighborhood who had boxed many a child's ear for walking on her grass. I wasn't going to be her next victim. I ran lickity split with the wind blowing on my face and through my long black hair. My head felt so hot, I thought I would be sick to my stomach. I was almost home.

Finally, I saw my mother sitting on the porch swing awaiting my arrival. As soon as she saw me, the serene look upon her face turned to one of horror. She shot inside the house and quickly returned, sprinting toward me, and carrying a blanket. Confused and frightened, I began to cry and ran my fingers through my long hair. A shock of pain ran through my hand. I realized my hair was on fire!

Grabbing me with all her might, Mama threw me into the long pleats of her skirt and then threw the blanket over us both. I could feel her hands twisting, and turning, and thrashing, and slapping through the dark folds of the blanket. The burning sensation penetrated deep into my scalp. As though we could both stand no more, my mother gently hugged me and fell to her knees and wept.

Unveiling the blanket from my head, there was an incredible stench. As I looked into my mother's eyes, I could tell she also was in great pain. Blisters were rising on her hands and forearms. She suffered worse than I did. I detested fire at that moment. I hated myself more for striking that match.

The doctor was summoned. My mother's arms had sustained second degree burns. Large bandages were bound loosely on both her arms and had to be changed frequently. The doctor said it would take two weeks for her to fully recover, and she would be unable to accomplish her daily tasks for at least several days. I suffered only minor burns on my scalp and fingers. In fact, I still had half of my waist length hair. It was at that moment, more than ever before, I knew of my mother's love for me. She would have gladly given her life for mine, and I knew my only wish was that I could bear the pain for her. There was no adequate punishment for my stupidity. Just the silent recognition in my heart of the agony I had caused her. It weighed on my soul as a ton of lead.

Chapter Nine - Best Friends

It was springtime in 1910. The discovery of oil in this part of Oklahoma had produced a booming economy. The west end of Enid was developing, so my father bought a home on West Broadway. It was a large and lovely home with many bedrooms and a sprawling front porch. Jimmy was back home, and it was wonderful to have him here. He was delivering mail, studying law, and helping Papa at the courthouse. He was busy. His head was always buried in law books. I didn't see him much, except in the evenings. Jimmy was sensitive and kind and was courting a wonderful girl named Laura. I held my oldest brother in highest regard.

Some of our best friends, the Drummonds, lived across the street. Betsy had been my friend for several years, and we were as close as ever. She owned a new bright red bicycle, and I wanted one too. Because I was accident prone, Papa was afraid I'd hurt myself, and my recent request for a new bike had been firmly denied.

Despite the disappointment of not getting a bike, I was feeling chipper today. Mama was going to buy me an Easter bonnet. A spanking NEW Easter bonnet! I had never worn a new bonnet - just the ole hand me downs from my sisters. For weeks, I had been eyeing a particular bonnet at the store. It had little pink satin rosebuds and long pink ribbons streaming down the back. This is the bonnet I really wanted. I prayed it would not be too expensive for Mama to purchase

Mama and I rode the streetcar to the square. It was very convenient now because it ran next to our house. We each paid five cents and boarded. I felt important because I had a purposeful destination. We arrived at the store, and to my relief, the bonnet was still there. I grabbed it off the shelf. "Mama! Mama! This is the one I want." Mama looked at the price tag and sighed, weighing the decision in her mind. Finally, she smiled and said, "Janey, it's yours." I gave her a big hug and smiled in delight. Mama paid for the bonnet with the last bit of change in her purse, and we walked home. I felt like I was walking on air as I envisioned myself in my Easter finery.

My thoughts turned to Betsy and I wondered if she would be impressed. The Drummonds had a grand home full of elegant furniture. The Drummond girls, Betsy and Maribelle, were seldom denied anything they requested. Their wardrobes were exquisite, and they always wore the latest fashion. However, I doubted even Betsy would have a bonnet as beautiful as mine!

Upon arriving home, I bounced up the stairs and removed my bonnet from the hatbox. I put it on and paraded around the house feeling elegant! Soon, Mama's voice was calling me. Betsy was at the door. I stashed the hat. I greeted Betsy from the top of the stairs, "Betsy, come on up, I have something to show you!" Betsy rushed up the stairs and was breathing heavily when she reached the top. I popped out from behind my bedroom door and said, "Boo! What do you think of my beautiful new bonnet?" Her eyes grew round, and her face turned sour. "Janey, she sighed, "You look like the devil in that hat!" I couldn't believe my ears. I was crushed. My anger exploded, and I verbally retaliated, "Betsy! You have RED hair!" I slammed my bedroom door, and I heard Betsy running down the stairs and out the front door.

I threw the bonnet across the room and fell sobbing onto my bed. How could Betsy be so mean and hateful? I sobbed louder. I felt Mama's gentle presence as she patted my shoulder. "Janey, what is this uproar all about?" she asked. I replied, "Betsy said I looked like the devil in my Easter Bonnet!" Mama asked, "What did you say to her?" I replied, "I told her, she had red hair!" Mama choked back laughter, "Oh, Janey that's terrible!"(as she bit the side of her cheek to keep from laughing) "The Drummonds are our very good friends. Pull yourself together and go make up with Betsy this afternoon."

I knew Mama was right. I washed my face and put on some fresh powder, slipped on a clean midi-blouse, and buttoned up my shoes. I left the house dreading the heavy task of reconciliation. As I knocked on the door, Betsy was peeking out the window from behind the curtains. With a squeamish expression, she slowly opened the door. With a deep breath I sighed, "I'm sorry Betsy, I don't want you to be angry with me, I know you don't like my bonnet." She replied, "Oh Janey, that is the most wonderful bonnet I have ever seen, and you looked beautiful wearing it. You see, yesterday, I bought one identical to it!"

After her confession, we both giggled. "I bet you look outstanding in your hat too! Oh please model it for me," I suggested. Betsy replied, "Stay here, my room is a mess." Before long she pranced into the room wearing a gorgeous dress and the bonnet to match. Gulping down my pride was like choking on a large piece of coal. Yet, I managed to sputter, "Betsy you look as lovely as a picture of springtime." Grinning from ear to ear, Betsy squeezed her arms tightly around me and she sang, "Friends

Forever…" Betsy then declared, "Let's go get ice cream, my treat." We skipped out the door hand in hand - friends for life. The raven and red headed girls.

Chapter Ten - The Miracle Medicine

Dr. Cotton was busy that summer making medical rounds as several children had contracted Typhoid fever. He and Dr. Fields were the only two doctors I knew growing up. I remember drinking from a well with putrid water. Although I spit the water out, I could not get rid of the foul taste in my mouth. Six days later, it struck me as I awoke. The dull aches in my arms and legs began to intensify. My stomach felt queasy, and my head felt hot.

My mother took one long look at me and sent me marching upstairs to bed. Dr. Cotton came in the late afternoon and, after a full examination, stated most definitely that I had contracted Typhoid fever. To better care for my needs, Mother moved my bed downstairs in a littler corner of the living room. Since the whole family had been exposed, no visitors were at the house. Dr. Cotton told us that no quarantine was necessary. However, visitors were discouraged.

It wasn't long before the sickness invaded my entire being. I couldn't recall the day or the hour. In my delirium, I wanted to go swim and run by the lake and be free. Instead, I sensed I was drowning in a swamp of dark gloomy sickness. I couldn't break through the surface where my family waited with outstretched arms. Oh, how I ached. My joints grew swollen and inflamed. The pain seemed more than I could manage.

My loving family attended to all my needs. They fluffed up my pillows, brought me cold rags, and held my head up while coaxing me to sip a little soup. When Papa came in after a long day's work, his shadow fell over my bed, and I could sense his strong presence. He gently held my hand and bowed his head to pray. Dr. Cotton warned Papa that I was growing weaker and that another child had perished from this disease. I sensed the heaviness of the household and began to fear for my life.

With wisps of hair stringing down her face and eyes sunken in fatigue, Mama kept vigil over my bed day and night. With each moan, my mother's heart grew heavier. She had given birth to me at the age of forty-- I was her seventh child. She had long grueling labors with no anesthesia, except for a little chloroform. Papa had been thrilled about the thought of another child, but Mama had dreaded her last pregnancy. Yet, now at the age of 10, without a second thought, I knew I had captured a special place in her heart even beyond that of my brothers and sisters.

I continued to decline, and I couldn't stand to have anyone touch me. Mother and Irene wrapped me in cold sheets to stop my raging fever. I knew Mama sensed I might be dying. She knelt beside my bed, held my hand, and whispered, "My dearest Janey, if you should pass, I promise I will find some way to communicate with you after death."

Morning broke and I still wasn't any better. Dr. Fields was standing by my bed feeling helpless when the phone rang. His colleague Dr. Cotton was calling to tell him about a drug that have been developed in Germany a few years before and that could now be obtained in Oklahoma City. Maybe it could help. Dr. Cotton volunteered to take the morning train to Oklahoma City to get it. Dr. Cotton returned later that evening with a bottle of tiny grey pills. I managed to swallow hard and to force one down. I will never forget that day, nor my family, because it was Bayer Aspirin that broke my fever and saved my life.

Chapter Eleven - Fattie Thatcher Will Get You

A rumor spread like wildfire among the town's children. At the very mention of Fattie Thatcher's name, a cold chill would crawl down your spine. Goose bumps would break out and the little hairs on your arms would stand up. When a child did something naughty, other children would quickly threaten, *"Fattie Thatcher will get you!"* Fattie Thatcher was the biggest, fattest, meanest policeman in town.

Fattie was a bald and most unbecoming man who wore a constant scowl. He lived alone by the railroad tracks in a ramshackle, broken down house with no windows. He always spoke in a gruff low voice and never had a kind word to say. Almost every day he chased after and yelled at children. If we happened to pass him on the streets, we would shuffle by in terror straining our necks in the opposite direction to avoid eye contact. Fattie would call after us loudly, "Don't be naughty or I'll come to get ya!" We would scream and run for our lives. The thought of being arrested by Fattie Thatcher was a fate worse than death.

On this day, I did something I knew positively I should not do. I played with the girl from the forbidden family. My parents had strictly instructed all of the Cullison children not to interact with anyone from this family. This was not a matter of superior status but simply one of hygiene. Everyone in Enid knew that the members of this family were often infested with head lice and always slow to seek a remedy.

I saw her skipping down by the railroad tracks. She smiled at me in such an engaging way and invited me to come play with her. Before I realized what I was doing, my friendly nature took over, and I ran to say hello. She had a sweet face but appeared terribly unkempt and dirty. I felt sorry for her bedraggled condition. I had planned just to chat for a moment, but soon found myself engrossed in teaching her how to make "funny money." I explained that by putting pennies on the railroad tracks and waiting for a train to run over them, she could make her pennies three times bigger with Abe Lincoln's face stretched out in the funniest way. That is why I called it "funny money." The little girl, whose name I never knew, bent close to me as I laid several pennies on the track to carry out my demonstration.

Just then. I heard my brother Douglas calling, "Janey, Janey." When I turned to look, he was standing about 30 feet away looking at me in disgust. "Janey, you come home this instant!" he sternly demanded. Like a slap to the head, I instantly remembered the prohibition that I had violated. I was playing with the little girl from the "forbidden family." Douglas walked quickly up to me and jerked me by the elbow. Knowing I was in big trouble, I turned to go home half waving goodbye to the forbidden girl.

All the way home, Douglas threatened to call Fattie Thatcher. I pleaded with him to reconsider, but he had no mercy. As we approached the house, he yelled, "Mother! Mother! Janey was playing with the family with the head lice." I expected the worst and received it well. Mama jumped on me like the plague and fussed at me all the way to the tub. I was stripped. My clothes were put into a big pot for boiling, and I was plopped into the tub like a contaminated object. Mama vigorously scrubbed my body and washed my hair until my skin was raw and my scalp throbbed.

After the humiliating wash down, I was struck with fear that Douglas might have really called Fattie Thatcher. I wanted to ask Douglas. But, if I asked and he had forgotten, it would only prompt him to carry out his devious plan. Instead, I chose to go to bed in terror. I tossed and turned all night. My adrenaline flowed faster than the Colorado River, and my heart pounded in my chest. I was afraid to look out the window for fear that the gruesome face of Fattie Thatcher would appear.

Hope of sleep faded as these frightful thoughts continued to flood my mind. I was especially angry with Douglas for betraying his own flesh and blood! Suddenly, just as I was finally growing weary enough to doze off, the door creaked opened. There before me was Fattie Thatcher. Gasping for breath, terror gripped me like a rabbit awaiting the coyote's grasp. I was frozen and unable to breathe. I knew I would surely die.

As he moved closer, my hands tightly gripped the bedposts. I had heard stories about Fattie Thatcher carrying off the town drunks and chaining them to the paddy wagon. I was certain this would be my plight. With the last drop of courage I could muster, I looked up to see my tormenter face to face. Instead, I beheld the face of Irene. She had secured stuffed pillows in her night shirt with a belt and stuffed her hair into a cap. With no other intention than to scare the tee-waden out of me, she had conspired with Douglas to impersonate Fattie Thatcher. "How wicked!

How cruel!" First Douglas and now Irene - betrayed by my favorite brother and sister.

I screamed in a shrill voice and burst into tears. Irene drew back realizing she had gone too far. Papa sprang into the room to see what was wrong. At first perplexed by my tears and Irene's strange get-up, he quickly assessed the situation. Papa glared at Irene and ordered her to her room. Papa then lovingly took me in his arms and held me close. In the embrace of my father, I calmed down.

To relieve the terror of this night, I reached into my heart to find the answer that had always been hidden there - the absolute never wavering voice. Comforting me in my sorrow, strengthening me in my weakness, giving me peace in my terror - even beyond my father's arm were the words of love, the holy words of God… "Peace I leave with you. My own peace I give you. Not as the world gives do I give you. Do not be troubled or afraid." It soothed my soul like a sweet melody. Just as dawn was breaking, I finally nestled down into my pillows and slept. Never again would Fattie Thatcher's name grip my soul like ice. God was bigger than Fattie. I knew if it came right down to it, God would defend me against Fattie Thatcher or give me the power to defend myself. My night of fear was finally over, and I had found the true peace I needed at last.

Chapter Twelve - Going South

The August morning sunlight streamed through my window, and I jumped out of bed. It was a glorious Sunday morning, and I was excited. Today was the day I was going on a train to visit my Aunt Margaret and my four cousins. It was 60 miles due south to El Reno - a long way for a ten-year old traveling by herself. The scent of buttermilk biscuits and coffee rose from the kitchen. My mother has been up since the cock crowed preparing our Sunday meal.

My father was a member of the Enid Methodist Church and was attending services with Jimmy. This church was constructed in 1909 and located on West Randolph Street several blocks from our house. Mama didn't go to church. A parish member had once asked her why. She explained it was because she wouldn't leave her children at home by themselves. When the parishioner said, "The Lord will take care of them," my mother snapped back: "Yes, and I am going to be there to see that HE does!" That exchange left the parishioner speechless but greatly tickled my mother's funny bone. After all, she didn't believe in forcing children to sit in hard wooden pews for long hours listening to words that flew above their heads. She believed her children were better off seeking God whenever they convened with nature and His creation.

Papa and Jimmy returned home at noon. Sunday dinner was delightful! Buttermilk biscuits, fried chicken, black eyed peas, and fresh cucumbers that my mother had grown herself. She always set the table with our finest linen tablecloth. My mother had brought it from Iowa in a wagon. June told me that she had used this same tablecloth when the family lived in a primitive dugout in Kansas. I concluded that my mother must have been an elegant woman no matter where she went or what trying circumstances she faced.

Irene's new beau, Michael Smith, was very handsome with his brown hair and sparkling blue eyes. He wore a topcoat with a stiff white shirt as he sat at the table. But poor Michael had a stuttering problem. And when he was around my father, his nervousness increased making his stuttering worse. My brother Douglas, possibly to provoke a situation, looked at Michael and asked about his sick horse. Alarmed he had to speak, Michael turned bright red and replied, "The h-h-horse ju-just pa-pa-pa-pa-aaast away." There was silence. I knew if I dared laugh, my parents would give me the thrashing of my life. I truly felt sorry for Michael and his stuttering, but I still found this episode hilarious.

I bit my tongue and held my breath to suppress the laughter. Milk rose from my throat and poured through my nose all over the linen tablecloth. Choking, I fled from the room and burst through the back door into freedom. I fell on the ground and began to laugh out loud. I was forced to suppress my laughter again when I saw Mama coming out the back door. I took the glass of water from her hands and drank heartily. Mama expressed concern that I had become sick at the table. I reassured her it was just a piece of bread caught in my throat. She patted my back and sent me upstairs to finish packing for my trip. I heard her chuckling as she walked away, and I wondered if she knew the real reason for my exit from the table.

We arrived at the station with just a few minutes to spare. I boarded the train in my Sunday best, a bright blue calico, midi-length dress with two laced-trimmed petticoats underneath and bonnet to match. I was very impressed with myself being a 10-year old traveling alone to a distant town. It made me feel like a sophisticated adult. The train car was half empty. The windows were cracked, and the warm dusty air was blowing in. The rocking sensation and warmth made me drowsy. I sat alone watching the tumbleweeds skipping and dancing over the red Oklahoma clay.

After about 30 minutes, I became restless. I began to imagine that I was a gorgeous widow, alone and mysterious, traveling in a foreign country. I peeked in the brown sack my mother had packed. There was a peppermint stick, some cookies, and paper, pen and ink. I wasn't hungry, so I retrieved the paper, pen and ink. I had to be very careful not to spill ink on my new blue calico dress. Carrying on my fanciful charade as the imaginary widow, I wrote:

> *"Dear Sir; I am a beautiful, young widow alone in a strange country. I am searching for an eligible bachelor to court me with intentions of marriage. I have been very lonely since the death of my beloved William; God rest his soul. Please contact me. You will not be disappointed. My address is West Broadway Avenue in Enid. Sincerely yours, Jeannette C. Cullison*

The train pulled into the El Reno station precisely at 4:00 pm. As I looked out the window, I spied my jolly Aunt Margaret and my cousins waving and jumping up and down to get my attention. I threw the letter aside and bounced gaily off the train. I was soon smothered with hugs

47

and kisses. Aunt Margaret threw my luggage in the horse drawn buggy, and we all jumped in. Aunt Margaret grabbed the reins and yelled, "giddy up!" And off we rode to their farm.

Chapter Thirteen - Failure in the Kitchen

Aunt Margaret was my father's younger sister. She had a merry Irish disposition but was very strict. She decided that I had been granted too much freedom roaming the Oklahoma prairies and had been left to my mischief too long. Therefore, she declared it was time for me to "have the reins pulled in" and to learn some womanly chores in the kitchen.

Aunt Margaret sat about to teach me how to bake bread, and I was less than eager to learn. The outside August heat was almost unbearable, and it was even worse inside the kitchen. But I smiled in compliance and pretended to enjoy this baking lesson. Aunt Margaret stirred the flour and eggs and sprinkled in the yeast. She taught me how to knead the dough and divide it into two tidy loaves - ready to bake.

I kneaded, pulled and twisted until my arms ached. I divided the dough. The two loaves lay before me, and now I had the boring task of watching the bread rise. Aunt Margaret and my cousins left for town, and I was entrusted to complete this remaining task alone. I considered this a most unpleasant chore.

After what seemed an eternity, one loaf of bread finally rose. However, the other one did not. It just sat there - a big blob of lumpy dough. Oh, what would I do? I suspected Aunt Margaret would not be pleased. I pondered my options as I gazed out the window. Then, as if a light went on in my head, I saw it… a big mound of soft dirt in the back yard. I thought to myself, "I'll just bury the dough." I took the defective loaf outside and soon it disappeared. It was buried and out of sight forever - so I thought.

Aunt Margaret came home and was pleased to see one lovely loaf of bread. I was relieved that she forgot to ask about the second loaf. She was soon distracted teaching me other chores in the kitchen. The late afternoon sun continued to beat down all around the house. As I glanced out the kitchen window, I noticed the mound of dirt in the backyard expanding.

The growing dirt attracted curious animals. First a dog came sniffing and pawing until this unusual phenomenon scared him away. Then came two cats pouncing and playing upon the rising dirt. Finally, Uncle John, who was working in the nearby shed, took notice and sauntered over to inspect. Perplexed, he retrieved a shovel from the shed with the intention of killing whatever thing was making this happen. He plunged the shovel into the ground and a burst of white goo exploded into the air. My uncle stood startled with sticky dough dangling from his nose and stuck all over his clothes. His head slowly turned toward the house, and he saw me peering through the window in horror. A smile appeared on his face, and he burst into laughter. He had correctly deduced what had happened after my failure in the kitchen. He raised his finger to his lips as if to say, "hush!" He would keep my secret safe. I smiled back my million-dollar smile.

My visit in El Reno continued for a week. Aunt Margaret exposed me to many more domestic lessons. I also found time to be with my dear cousins. We played many games running upon the farm and told stories while sitting in the haystacks in the barn. It was truly a wonderful and delightful time. I also developed a special fondness for my Uncle John. He never did tell Aunt Margaret about his strange backyard discovery.

Chapter Fourteen - The Calling Suitor

As I boarded the train to come home, I was tired but content. I curled up in my seat as the sun cast warm rays upon my head. The motion of the train rocked me fast asleep. I awoke to a loud whistle and the conductor calling, "Enid, this stop, Enid!" Lazily, I pulled myself up and stumbled toward the exit. My father and mother were there to meet me. My heart lurched toward them, and I ran into their arms.

Papa retrieved my bags, we mounted our wagon, and Nellie briskly pulled us home. Our grand white house soon appeared, and I admired the blossoming colors within my father's flower garden. It was wonderful to be home in the refuge of my own domain. My father returned to the courthouse, and my mother unpacked my clothes. I recounted with Mama the highlights of my visit to El Reno. She laughed heartily when I told her about my baking lessons.

Mama went to the kitchen to prepare dinner. The telephone rang. Seeing how calls were never for me, I took great delight in answering. A deep, slow male voice inquired, "Jeanette Cullison?" Quite surprised, I replied, "This is she." After a long pause, the gentleman explained he had been traveling on a train and came across something belonging to me. "It was a letter," he said. I gasped. Oh my soul, that letter! With the address provided in the letter, he had been able to have the operator connect him to our home.

Terror gripped me. In heartfelt words, this caller told me that my letter had deeply touched him and that he had thought of nothing else but me -- the poor lonely widow on her quest for happiness. Then the words came I dreaded most, "We might be well suited for one another, and I hope I can soon make your acquaintance." Oh, good grief! He wants to meet me. I began to panic. My first impulse was to lie and tell him I had already met another man of my dreams. But when I opened my mouth, I could not lie. The debate within my conscience ended, and I decided to tell the truth.

After taking a long gulp, I replied in a quivering voice, "I'm awfully sorry, I'm so, so terribly sorry, but I'm just a little girl ten years old. I was bored on the train, so I made the letter up." Embarrassment overwhelmed me, and my cheeks began to flush. Even my ears grew hot. After a pause, I heard a slight chuckle on the other end of the receiver, "Well, young lady, you have quite an imagination. I hope you have learned a lesson." I promptly replied, "I assure you, sir, that I have… Good-bye." He hung up.

I was staring at the wall in disbelief. I slapped my face in shame. Oh, this poor man, I thought. How could I have been so stupid? I prayed no one else had overheard the conversation on the party line. "Janey! Janey!" I twirled around, and there was Irene. Had she heard? Would she tell? Could I endure the teasing for the rest of my life from my sister? Then Irene asked, "Who was on the phone?" I could only manage to sputter out, "Ughhh…" Irene then asked, "Was it Michael Smith calling for me?" "No," I replied firmly. "Why didn't you just say so, you silly goose," sparked Irene as she spun out of the room.

Rescued from calamity, I sighed in relief. The whole world would not have to know that I was the precarious little girl who masqueraded as a widow and wrote a letter to woo a new husband.

Chapter Fifteen - Judge Cullison and His Court Days

Each day after arriving home from work, Papa sat close to Mama on the divan. Douglas, May, Irene and me often formed a semi-circle at his feet listening intently as he described the events of the day. He shared about the court decisions he had made and his interactions with interesting people. Bible reading and prayer often followed these discussions. The white-haired judge spoke with authority and kindness. His judicial decisions altered the lives of men and women. Anointed with wisdom, he was greatly admired and respected by all.

When he ran for a seat on the Oklahoma Supreme Court a decade later, James Cullison explained his judicial philosophy: "A judge should never confer favors on friends or punish enemies. A judge should be controlled by the law and facts in the case. A judge who seeks notoriety by rendering popular opinions is an unsafe man. A judge who is not controlled by divine and human law will prove a failure." These were principles he followed every day.

With great anticipation, we awaited this evening for the Judge to share his stories of the day. He reported to us that the first case that day had involved a young Mexican man on trial for his life. This man had robbed a local bank and shot the banker dead. All the evidence screamed his guilt. After weighing punishment alternatives, my father sentenced him to life imprisonment instead of death. My father knew that Governor Lee Cruce would almost certainly commute any death sentence because of his strong opposition to capital punishment.

As the sentence was to be proclaimed, the young Mexican stood upright and proudly waited to receive his punishment. The white-haired judge brought down his gavel and pronounced: "Life imprisonment." Having been spared the death penalty, the man slumped his shoulders and sighed deeply. My father felt a pang of compassion and uttered, "Peace on you, sir." The Mexican looked up with a gnarled smile and replied, "Piss on you too, Judge." We had never heard our father use that sort of language and, in shock, we burst into hysteria! My mother squealed and held her sides, trying to contain her laughter.

Each day upon leaving the courthouse, Papa strolled home on Main Street passing Mr. Thomas on the sidewalk. Mr. Thomas was a big burly man with a booming voice. Abruptly, he would slap my father forcefully on the back and abrasively inquire, "How are you today Judge?" The jolt always stung Papa's shoulder and sometimes knocked his black derby hat to the ground, coating it with red dust. While Mr. Thomas had come to greatly enjoy this daily ritual, Papa had finally had enough.

After a very difficult case, my father was briskly walking along Main Street anxious to reach home. Looking up, he saw Mr. Thomas approaching. In his usual hearty voice Mr. Thomas boomed, "How are you, Judge?" But just as Mr. Thomas lifted his hand to strike Papa's shoulder, Papa's fuse burned short. He drew his fist in fury and belted Mr. Thomas to the ground. Astonished and shaken, Mr. Thomas collected himself and rose from the sidewalk. Quivering, he meekly sputtered, "Well, hell Judge, I was just kiddin'!" The Judge replied, "Well, hell Mr. Thomas, I was too!"

When that scene as shared by Papa would replay in my mind, a smile would always come to my face. There was an understanding reached between Mr. Thomas and Papa from that day forward - a truce of sorts. They were frequently seen laughing with one another. A bond of friendship had formed, and this comical memory of their encounters on Main Street was shared for years to come.

Chapter Sixteen - Another Episode with Douglas

On this quiet October afternoon, I was sitting and reading a book in my bedroom. The explosion rocked the house and knocked me from my chair. Black smoke billowed outdoors. My eyes burned as foul air began to flood the house. Disoriented, I couldn't imagine what had happened, and I rushed down to see. At the bottom of the stairs, my mother and I grabbed hands and bolted out the front door. Coughing from gulps of black smoke, we sought to regain our senses. As the thick smoke lifted from the yard, we frantically assessed the situation. Then I remembered about the old furnace that lay in the backyard in pieces.

Much to Papa's distress, the eyesore had grown on him like the plague, and he continually commanded, "Douglas get rid of that garbage!" Douglas would always ask, "How?' and Papa with the pressures of time, would reply sternly, "I don't care how, just get rid of it!" Douglas was full of ingenuity, and I could picture his brain contriving a plan. Douglas! The water heater! A plan for destruction! The pieces of the puzzle began to fit together.

Mama and I both realized in a flash that Douglas must have been responsible for this explosion. But where was he now? Was he still alive? In panic, we both screamed for Douglas only to hear the echo of the wind reply. When we reached the backyard, Douglas was laying on the lawn face down. "No!" I screamed. Mama drew her arm up to stop me from touching him. She knelt by his side, and tenderly ran her fingers through his reddish blonde hair. Then, as if God had heard Mama's prayer, Douglas moaned. Thank God, he was alive! Hope rose within me. I ran with all my strength to fetch Dr. Cotton. By the time I returned, Douglas had rolled over on his back. I realized his grave condition when I saw charred flesh peeling from his face.

Douglas' freckled face was swollen grotesquely. Blisters were forming all over, and his eyes remained closed as he drifted in and out of consciousness. We could see that he had burns all over his face, arms and hands. Mama and I knelt by him and prayed. Mama spoke words of comfort. This moment seemed suspended in time, and I feared that if it shattered, Douglas might leave us forever. Surely God would answer the pleas of our heart.

A crowd had gathered around us. Dr. Cotton put his hand on Mama's shoulder and knelt to treat Douglas. Dr. Cotton's troubled expression and heavy sighs did not lend encouragement. Yet I refused to believe Douglas would die. They carried him into the house and laid him on the bed. Papa, Mama and Dr. Cotton remained in the room, and the door was shut. From the room, we could hear the muffled utterances of a concerned conversation.

Mama emerged from the room looking like a ghost. She walked down the stairs as if in a trance to fill the wash bowl. Dr. Cotton stayed and treated Douglas through the night. Irene, May and I fell asleep in the drawing room fully clothed - one on the floor, one on the divan, and me in the chair. We hadn't meant to sleep, but the night drew long in waiting. The dawn broke, and we were eager to hear about Douglas.

Dr. Cotton slumped through the door of the room. It was hard to gauge his expression. He just looked exhausted. He nodded at us as he passed and walked out of the house. Papa came down and sunk into his chair. He told us Douglas had suffered serious burns over much of his body and was experiencing great pain. Douglas would be sleeping most of the time, and we would have to be quiet and continue to pray for his recovery.

Food appeared in our kitchen like magic. The neighbors brought a variety of delicious morsels embracing our family with love. Notes and letters of concern came pouring in. Our family was deeply touched by this display of affection from our community. Douglas' face was wrapped in bandages, and he lay very still. I was told he was receiving morphine for pain. Papa sat each day with Douglas with his head bent and his lips silently moving. I knew Papa was praying. Day by day, Douglas improved and gained strength. The burns were finally healing. We believed he was finally "out of the woods" and relief flooded us.

After a week or so, I grew weary of Douglas' constant demands. He asked for food. He asked for something to drink. And he always requested me to get it for him. Yet I would go each time, just as he asked, as I was so grateful that he was alive. At last, the final set of bandages was ready to be cast off. Though they had been changed frequently, none of us had seen Douglas' face except for Dr. Cotton. Fearful of what would appear, I breathed deeply. The last time I had seen, his face was grossly deformed by the burns. As the last bandage was discarded. Douglas turned to us, his face was glowing, pink and fresh. He still had the most beautiful baby skin I had ever seen! God had been good to us.

Douglas blew up the old furnace to rid the yard of its ugliness. He acquired the dynamite down at the railroad yard by means that were never fully explained. For Douglas, this was a simple and quick solution to a problem. He paid dearly for his foolishness and thereafter learned to weigh his decisions more carefully. But just as Papa had demanded, the backyard was rid of the hideous furnace.

Chapter Seventeen - A Childhood Wish

It was the season of pumpkin pies, frosty mornings, and scarlet leaves. Douglas was thrilled. He had joined the football team and wanted to make his little sister proud. He tried on his football uniform, and he gave me a mean look with a snarl! I burst into laughter and told him he was fierce. Douglas was almost six feet tall with sandy hair. He was quite a good- looking boy, and I knew several girls who thought so too.

This day was not for football. Our family had planned an autumn picnic at the park. I was glad my handsome older brother was coming along. Father hitched old Nellie to the buggy, and we were off to the park Most of the town convened there. We would spread our blankets on the dry brown grass, enjoy our delicious treats, and joyfully share about the events of our lives. The afternoon melted away.

I decided to play under Old Nellie. I was pretending to be a miniature horse for leprechauns. Old Nellie never seemed to get nervous, but would stare down at me, chew a bit of hay, and look annoyed. Then I'd rub her belly and she whinnied loudly. I thought I heard someone get into the buggy. Then it was obvious, as someone shouted, "Giddy up, old Nellie." Large buggy wheels began to turn toward me. Petrified, I froze as they jolted deep into my waist. I lost consciousness. My parents were frantic as they realized that I had briefly been pinned underneath the buggy. From what they relayed to me later, my mother screamed in horror and my father's face turned ashen grey. Douglas jumped from the wagon and gasped when he looked down and saw my crumpled body. My father ran like lightening to get Dr. Julian Fields.

Dr. Julian Fields, Papa, Mama, Irene, May, and Douglas formed a semi-circle around me as I lay next to the buggy. I was still unaware of my surroundings. But as if far away, I could hear faint voices whispering. The doctor bent down to examine me. He squeezed my hand and rhetorically asked in a gentle voice, "Oh, little girl, what can we do for you?" Suddenly, my senses returned. I opened my eyes brightly and replied, "I think I'd feel better if I had some ice cream." There was a moment of silence followed by gasps of relief. My family was shaken back to the reality that I was very much alive and well enough to ask for ice cream.

"Oh Jeannette!" my mother cried. Father patted perspiration off his forehead as they extended a hand to pull me to my feet. They gave me a gentle hug and we walked back into the house. My father's face remained ashen and my mother's hand trembling at the thought of what could have been.

I felt a little queasy and light-headed as I sank into my bed. However, after sleeping several hours, I felt as fresh as a daisy on a spring morning. On the other hand, my dear mother had gone to bed with one of her "sick headaches" that would taunt her for days. She had them occasionally, and we knew not to disturb her when her door was shut. The room was kept dark because the light hurt her eyes and intensified the headaches.

While Mama recovered, I passed my time sewing new undergarments and crocheting the lace edging around my panties. I struggled, and my handiwork was sloppy compared to May's. When she finally rebounded from her migraine headache, Mama came into the room. Upon inspecting my earnest but flawed efforts, she reassured me, "It could not be seen on a galloping horse." This was one of her favorite sayings. It always added a forgiving note to my faux pas and helped me to deal in life with my many imperfections.

Chapter Eighteen - The New Car

Papa longed to own a car. The contraptions were becoming quite popular in this growing town. Enid's population had reached over 10,000 people. Old Nellie was getting along in years and it was necessary to replace her with another horse or a new car. Papa decided he would try a Model T Ford. This newly introduced car was big, black and shiny. It was finally here and ready for a test drive. My heart raced with excitement with the thought of owning this magnificent machine.

We watched from the front porch as Papa climbed in and cranked up the engine. Black exhaust poured from the tailpipe, and the engine rumbled. As the car jerked forward, Papa's face lit with excitement. Around and around the house he drove. Each time he passed by, we waved and yelled, "hurrah" with gusto. After about thirty minutes, the excitement died down and the expression on my father's face grew weary. We remained on the porch squinting in the sun and wondering when the test drive would end. But Papa continued to drive the car around and around.

It suddenly dawned on us that Papa could not stop the car. His facial expression was now one of total exasperation. He was a prisoner of this big black machine, and we wondered if he would ever escape. It was as if he was trapped in time perpetually circling the house. Finally, with a chug-chug-chug-bbb-pst, the car engine sputtered and died. It was out of gas! My father emerged from the car sighing and wiping perspiration from his forehead. He swore in that moment that he would never own a new car or try one again.

In those days, we walked almost everywhere. Our legs were firm and strong. We would travel by foot for miles and never think twice about it. Walking was not just for exercise but absolutely necessary. The streetcar offered an occasional option, and we would save our pennies to ride for enjoyment. Sometimes, if the distance was far, we would hitch up old Nellie and ride to our destination in our buggy.

Times were changing. New inventions that we had only read about were now realities in our community. The conveniences of modern necessity propelled us to adopt new ways of living. We knew that, despite his initial aversion to the unstoppable car, Papa would come around. If fact, in the years to come, Papa would buy several shiny new cars. The first one was this Model T-Ford of which we all became very proud.

Chapter Nineteen - Quarantined

It was early spring of 1911. I awoke one morning knowing something was terribly wrong. My head was burning with fever. My throat was sore. My stomach ached. As the day progressed, my face became flush red, and a pinkish rash appeared on my stomach.

Mama called Dr. Fields (we were becoming good friends) who promptly diagnosed my illness and nailed a sign upon our front door that read: *"Quarantined - Scarlet Fever."* There was no vaccine for scarlet fever. Dr. Fields instead made me drink a new serum made from the blood of horses. It tasted horrid, but Dr. Fields said it would help me recover.

May and Irene quickly evacuated the premises to stay with friends. No one else could leave or enter our home. My mother, father, Douglas and I were confined to the walls of our household. Mother had lost a child to whooping cough at the age of two, so every childhood illness brought a new sense of gripping fear.

Mrs. Godschalk left a large container of her hot matzo ball soup on our back porch. At first, this soup tasted strong and hearty, but by the third day, I was too weak to swallow. I was aching all over, depleted of all energy, and delirious with fever. My parents wrapped me in cool wet rags to bring the fever down. I recall hearing far away voices and seeing only blurry things when I tried to open my eyes.

Mrs. Lang, who lived behind us, begged my mother to allow her to come and pray for me. Mrs. Lang was a dear lady. but nobody was quite sure what religion she practiced. My mother relented hoping that a spiritual remedy would prove more effective than the nasty tasting serum

I had taken days before. Mrs. Lang scurried to my bedside, fell on her knees, and placed her hands on me to pray. Her powerful prayers evoked a keen spiritual awareness in me as I felt the complete presence, peace and comfort of God.

Gradually the illness ran its course. My strength and sense of awareness slowly improved each day. I was so thankful to my mother who had kept vigil over my bedside for two weeks. I was thankful for caring neighbors like Mrs. Godschalk and Mrs. Lang. But, mostly, I was thankful to God who had delivered me again from the brink of death.

The quarantine sign was removed. Then came the daunting task of disinfecting the house. Everything had to be aired and scrubbed. My sheets and bedding were boiled. Exhaustion swept over my mother as if an ocean wave caught her in its grasp and sent her crashing to the shore. As weak as I was, I sensed her frailty too. When the last chore was finished, she retired to her room for days. I was left in the care of my older sisters, May and Irene. We were very blessed as the disease had not spread through the family but had only infected me.

June returned home for the weekend after I recovered. She brought a priceless treasure, "Pearl Cream." It was a total wonder, as we were all very pale and freckle faced. The cream was intended to dissolve freckles. I was constantly reminded to wear my bonnet as the sun seemed to coax my pesky freckles out of hiding.

Mr. Otjen came to call on June and brought a surprise. He knew I had been sick. He called my name from the other end of the house. I arose and came blundering down the staircase. I wondered with excitement about what this could be. Mr. Otjen brought with him a lovely decorated box with a pink ribbon tied so pretty around it, "Janith," he said "I have a little gift for you." "It is as pretty and precious as you are." I blushed and a wave of shyness crept over me before I spoke, "Oh, Mr. Otjen, you are so kind to think of me, thank you so much."

The eager moment of discovery came as I untied the pink ribbon and lifted the cardboard lid. There before me were fifty little dolls, no bigger than my thumb. Perfect porcelain heads with tiny lace bonnets were mounted on their shoulders. The tiny dolls showcased intricate features as even their tiny blue eyes were delicately painted. "Mr. Otjen" I squealed, "These are penny dolls!" I had looked at them once at the Herzberg's Department Store. Pretty, precious, and perfect, the dolls were lined up row after row. I felt so privileged to own them! How the hours would fly when I lay underneath our cottonwood tree, sprawled out on a blanket, and pretending to be a head mistress of an orphanage.

As spring proceeded toward summer, Mr. Otjen's intentions grew serious for June. I was told they were to be married in several months. Nobody was happier than I. My heart fluttered with excitement at the thought of a wedding. My father was exuberant as Mr. Otjen was a young attorney with whom he shared so much in common. My mother immersed herself with wedding plans but looked a little wistful at the thought of losing a daughter. The pressure was in full swing! The wedding had to be big, expensive, and perfect for June. She was the oldest girl and the first child to marry. These festivities would make the Cullison family proud and give our community something special to remember.

Chapter Twenty - The Lost Treasure

My dear and favorite aunt was arriving from Kansas City on the one o'clock train, and I was thrilled! She would be staying two full weeks until the end of June. She wore her long dark hair twisted and braided on top of her head. Her eyes were as blue as the summer sky, and her features were dainty. Aunty told me she had a special place reserved for me in her heart. Being the extravagant one from my father's family, she wore a big brilliant diamond ring on each hand. She dressed in the finest clothes and was consumed by the fashion trends of the times. I couldn't believe she had been married three times and was currently without a husband. This was scandalous!

When she stepped off the train, she projected elegance. The world was always new to her as each day presented an adventure waiting to happen. How I adored her, and Mama loved her her too – although my mother never quite understood her ways. Our family loyalty was stronger than any such differences. Aunty told vivid stories about her husbands and the places she had lived. She desired to educate me about the wiles of womanhood. No one had more experience than one with so many husbands. My imagination of future romance was energized by these conversations, and the days flew by.

Life in our household that late spring mostly revolved around June's upcoming wedding to Mr. Otjen. Aunty shared her extravagant ideas for the wedding with Mama, and Mama would gently blow them off. As Mama carefully handwrote each wedding invitation, she reminisced about her own wedding. Mama had been eighteen and Papa nineteen when he proposed to her on a sleigh ride one moonlit wintry night. Mr. Otjen also desired the best for his bride. With the promise of love and hope for the future, he built a bungalow for June – it would be their first home. May was going to sing at the wedding. She sang for almost every wedding in town, and Irene would play the piano.

I soon grew weary of all this wedding talk. June demanded so much from my parents – seemingly squeezing every nickel from their pockets. Even paying for the five-dozen sugar cookies that Mrs. Flanigan made each week became a challenge - and that was only a dollar. When Mama passed our living room painting that depicted a raging sea, she cried out a verse from Alfred Lord Tennyson, "Break, break, break upon the cold grey rocks, oh sea." Then, walking a few more steps, she stopped and added her own verse, "You can break, break, break all you want to, but you will never be as broke as me." Mama chuckled to herself and moved on.

On this evening, after a delicious supper of hot cornbread, chicken, and fried okra, the family gathered in the drawing room to play and sing for Aunty. The Cullisons shared a great love for music. We loved to perform together as a family, and this was a special occasion. We sang gospel hymns, and Irene and May harmonized. People driving by in their buggies stopped to listen. This inspired us to sing even louder as we were full of pride for our music.

Aunty loved our performances, and she clapped and cheered with delight. That made me treasure her company even more. After we sang, Papa smoked his cigar and read verses from our big family Bible. We concluded this joyful evening by bowing our heads and reverently thanking the Lord for our lives.

The next morning brought a bright and glorious Oklahoma sky. I woke in anticipation of spending another day with Aunty. Mama was again confined to her room with one of her "sick headaches." She pulled the curtains closed so the sun wouldn't hurt her eyes. While I was sad Mama could not join us, I delighted in knowing I was taking Aunty to the library in which Mama took such pride. This was the first library in our town. Mama worked diligently with several other women from Enid to open it. She helped raise funds from other Enid citizens, and she ordered the library's first books from New York and Chicago.

Aunty was independent. She drove the buggy to the library with me sitting proudly beside her. Aunty adored the library. The building was filled with the aroma of new pine wood. The small building with its limited stacks of books was humble, but it represented a great accomplishment for Mama. After spending 30 minutes looking through several books, we left to go to the square.

As we passed the Grand Avenue Hotel, I told Aunty about a recent book that had been written about John Wilkes Booth. This book reported that John Wilke Booth had secretly lived at the Grand Avenue Hotel under the assumed name of David E. George. The book also reported that he committed suicide by poisoning himself. I was fascinated that Abraham Lincoln's assassin might have really lived in our town.

When we arrived at the square, we stopped to view the courtyard. The trees were a little taller this year and the grass seemed greener. As we paused, her hand in mine, I glanced down, and her diamonds caught my eye. It was as if a thousand little stars twinkled in the stones. I told Aunty how much I loved her diamonds and how I could hardly wait to own one myself. This prompted Aunty to pull her little black-tie purse from under the buggy seat. She dug to the bottom of the purse and pulled out a little box.

As she opened the box, I saw a beautiful antique Victorian diamond. I was spellbound and unable to look away. In the sunlight, I could see all the brilliant colors of the rainbow glittering in the stone. Then, without hesitation, Aunty presented it to me, "This is yours Janey. I didn't love the man who gave it to me, so it holds no sentiment. But if I give it to you, the stone will become precious to me." I was overwhelmed as Aunty continued to explain the purpose of this gift, "You see, when something is given without love, its beauty will not abound until one that is loved receives it with joy. You are the one I choose to receive it."

My mind could scarcely absorb the gift. I was now the owner of a priceless jewel. I was not even a woman, yet I felt like the secrets of womanhood must be trapped within this diamond. This valuable diamond was mine to treasure forever! My thoughts turned to protecting and preserving it. Where would I hide it? What would I do with it? When I grew up, how would I wear it? These thoughts consumed me.

When Mama heard that I had received this expensive and elaborate gift, she nearly choked. She pleaded with Aunty to reconsider or to at least surrender it to her for safe keeping. These pleas fell upon deaf ears as Aunty insisted that I keep the diamond ring. I adamantly promised that I would be responsible for its safe keeping. With a heavy sigh, my mother rolled her eyes and shrugged her shoulders. Aunty's merry blue eyes met mine. She winked, and I winked back. We had won, and Mama's understanding for her sister-in-law had grown even more remote.

Aunty's trip was coming to an end, and she would be leaving in the morning. The events of the past two weeks flooded my mind. All the wonderful conversations, the special family music, and, now, this most dazzling gift that a young girl could ever receive. How I would miss her. My heart became heavy and a few tears leaked from my eyes. Only God knew when I might see my Aunty again. She left early the next day before I arose - somehow it seemed easier that way.

To renew my spirits after Aunty's departure, I called Betsy Drummond and asked her to meet me at the square. I told her my Aunty had given me a special gift, and I wanted her to see it. I knew she would be flabbergasted seeing my diamond. I also suspected she would be a little green with envy. I could hardly wait. I removed the little box from its secret hiding place and put it deep into my pocket. Approaching the square, I could see Betsy's red, curly hair bouncing as she walked toward me. As we met, she playfully demanded, "Show me this expensive gift that your aunt gave you. Is it a new dress, a petticoat, or a locket perhaps?" I smiled and replied, "This is what it is," as I pulled out the box to show her my priceless gem.

I was hovering three steps above the ground with prideful delight until I noticed, along with Betsy, there was nothing in the box. Suddenly I became numb. Panic overtook me. "Calm down, Janey, it will be okay."

Betsy tried to comfort me. "What was in the box anyway?" Betsy asked. "My diamond!" I whaled. Betsy replied in disgust, "A diamond! Who would give a child a diamond?" My temper flared. "My aunt gave me the diamond because… because… she trusted me with it and… and…" I couldn't finish my sentence, and I burst into tears. I had failed miserably by losing the diamond.

We searched for hours. Betsy finally went home. I had forgiven her for being so insensitive, and she was truly sorry after she saw the depth of my despair. Oh, how could I? I treaded slowly home. I felt like I was carrying a gigantic weight upon my shoulders. I was emotionally drained. I felt like a jellyfish - a big white disgusting glob. I was not the least bit anxious to break the news to Mama. Maybe I would wait until tomorrow.

The moment I walked through the door, Mama observed my demeanor and asked what was wrong. She read me so easily. I fell into her arms and sobbed. Hesitantly, I began to explain, "Mama….." Before I could get out another word, she asked, "You lost your diamond, didn't you Janey?" I plaintively replied, "Yes, Mama, I lost it."

I fully expected Mama to lecture me about the loss of valuables or to tell me, "I told you so." Instead, she held me tight and let me cry. Then she handed me a cool rag to wash my face. Kissing my forehead, she sent me upstairs. I pounced upon my bed and put a pillow over my head. Mama's silent comfort had placed a safe distance between the dreadful moment I discovered I had lost my diamond and where I was now. I would do my best to put it behind me. But the echoes of my carelessness haunted me for weeks and months to come. We never found that diamond, and we never told Aunty what had happened.

Chapter Twenty-One - June's Marriage

It was early September, and the wedding was finally here! June possessed all the loveliness a summer bride could contain. She had transformed before us. I never knew she was so beautiful. Her dress had wide puffy sleeves and a long flowing train. The elegance of her white gloves and lacey veil presented her as royalty. The house was full of roses, bursting with color - red, white, pinks, and yellows - their fragrance was as sweet as the day.

Mr. Otjen stood handsome and dashing waiting for his bride to join him. His dark, curly hair was neatly combed. June and Mr. Otjen, both fair and tall, stood surrounded by family, friends, roses and love. I brought the ring on a little satin pillow. I sensed that I was strolling through the gates of heaven and wanted to inhale it all. If only I could capture this divine moment forever. The cake was lacy white, and the lady-like little sandwiches we had carefully assembled disappeared before us. Celebration and gaiety danced in our midst!

After the guests left, the bride and groom retired to their bungalow. The family sat in the living room, silent, happy, yet I sensed something strange. It was a vacancy of sorts – the knowledge that June would never be a resident in this house again. Her clothes vanished and her closet was bare. I now perceived her differently - not as a nagging older sister but as somebody's wife. How content I was that the dear somebody was Mr. Otjen! If I had ever known his first name was, it didn't matter. To me, he would always remain the dashing Mr. Otjen.

We didn't see June for three days. When we did, she beamed with happiness. Mr. Otjen and June were going to buy the little grocery store. They would settle in the back of the store and rent out their cozy new bungalow. It would be an opportunity for me. I could go in and load up on candy. I could hardly wait. However, I wondered how June, in her arrogant ways, could ever be happy living in the back of the tiny store.

Chapter Twenty-Two - Helping Mrs. O'Banyion's Son

Mrs. O'Banyion came to our house each week to do the wash. Her skin was the color of coffee without the cream. I wanted to touch her hair. It seemed so fluffy, but I couldn't figure out how to do so without her noticing. On this day, Mrs. O'Banyion was discouraged. She didn't laugh or sing her glorious songs. She breathed heavy and sighed. Her eyes were misting up. Mama asked Mrs. O'Banyion if anything was wrong. Big tears began to fall freely down her face. Mama walked over and gently put an arm around Mrs. O'Banyion, "Tell me about it, Mrs. O'Banyion, I want to know," Mama inquired.

Mrs. O'Banyion spilled out a horrendous account about her son Harold. He had been arrested on dubious charges and then "sat on" by Fattie Thatcher. Harold had bad lungs. Mrs. O'Banyion feared that, having been seriously beaten, Harold might die without proper care. Rumors had spread across Enid that the jailers sometimes brutalized the coloreds. Mama knew enough to be certain that these rumors were true.

Mama grabbed her bonnet and turned to Mrs. O"Banyion, "We're going to see the Judge right now." With hope of help awakened, Mrs. O'Banyion replied, "Thank you Mrs. Cullison, God bless you and the Judge." She followed Mama all the way to the courthouse, cautious because it wasn't acceptable to walk side by side with a white woman.

Upon hearing of Harold's plight, the Judge promised Mrs. O'Banyion he would do all he could to help. My father was a man who put his faith and convictions ahead of public convention. When a friend had asked him about his philosophy in life, he responded: "I was taught that if I trust God and work hard, He would show me the way." For the rest of that afternoon, Mrs. O'Banyion washed our clothes in the big washboard tub grateful that someone cared.

When Mrs. O'Banyion finished her day's work, she returned to the "the hollow" on the east end of town. Enid was a segregated community. All colored children attended the Booker T. Washington School. Many freed slaves from the South had settled in Oklahoma during the 1889 land rush. The town of Douglas, about 20 miles southeast of Enid, was one of more than 50 all-black towns that had sprouted up across Oklahoma.

It was considered wholly improper for a white man to go to "the hollow." White men usually went there only to seduce young black girls with an offer of money. I was fascinated with the prospect of secretly going to this forbidden place. I deemed this a necessary expedition. After the events of the day, I could not rest until I had seen "the hollow" myself. I was fearful of going alone, but I knew it would be foolish to ask anyone to join me.

The time was right. It was late afternoon, and the air hung heavy with honeysuckle, sweet and perfumed. Because my mother was resting from a headache, I knew she would not miss me. I quietly sneaked out the back door. I headed quickly toward "the hollow" with my heart beating fast. It took much longer to get there than I expected. My heart was heavy as I watched the colored people who worked in our town migrating back home. It was commonly understood by Whites and Blacks that the coloreds had to be out of the town by sundown.

With the hot September sun beating upon their heads, they trudged along to get to their humble homes. Fraught with exhaustion from a hard day's work, many sang along the way with their distinctive voices ringing out. I could now see small cluttered houses and ramshackle huts in the distance. There were no painted shutters or flower gardens. These homes were stark and bare. They stood row after row like surrendered soldiers, tattered and worn.

As I came closer, I saw Mrs. O'Banyion standing on a porch. I surmised this must be her home. I slithered into a row of bushes next to the house and crouched to listen. I heard low and muffled voices coming from the porch, and one sounded distinctly familiar. I shuffled a little closer in the bushes so I could hear what was being said. There was a man talking to Mrs. O'Banyion. When I peeked to see who it was, I saw the black suit, the stiff white shirt, and the black derby. The image of my father standing there snapped sharp in my mind as a photo.

The Judge took no notice of me, and I prayed he would not. Growing uncomfortable in the scratchy shrubs, I could not imagine what he was doing there. But then I heard him explain, "Mrs. O'Banyion, Harold is facing some serious charges, but I have arranged for him to get proper care at the jail tonight and to be released into your custody tomorrow." Ms. O'Banyion sighed in relief. The Judge continued, "After he is released, I have arranged for Harold to work in the garden of one of our neighbors and to keep their lawn. I believe Harold is a good young man who needs a job for which he can take pride and fill his hours."

The worry disappeared from Mrs. O'Banyion's face. She smiled for the first time that day, and expressed her gratitude, "Oh, thank you and bless your soul, Judge. You're a good man. Your wash will be cleaner than it ever has been." The Judge's face melted into a smile. He tipped his hat in respect and headed home. He walked with purpose in every step. He did not see me hiding in the shrubs, and I waited several minutes before following him home.

The Judge had acted upon his conscience and risked his reputation for justice. In an era that unfairly demanded that coloreds be treated differently, he knew no such prejudice. In his sight, a man was a man regardless of color or creed. My heart swelled with pride. This man of great courage and righteousness was my dear father.

Chapter Twenty-Three - The Birth of Little Mary

It was April 1912. The aroma of fresh paint and newly cut wood lingered through our growing township. The early vision of our community members was now fully materializing. It was an exciting time to live in a new town, a new state, with high hopes and kindred hearts. It made for an occasion to join our neighbors in celebration over this new land.

Mr. Otjen had rented the bungalow and had built June a new home with a small store in the front. It contained all the necessities for a young couple as well as a few odds and ends. The glass candy jars attracted my attention. The red licorice and peppermint shown through the glass coaxing my salivating expectations. Often, in payment for some little chore, June and Mr. Otjen allowed me to fill my pockets with candy. This candy became my treasure. Nothing like the precious diamond I had lost, but I still took great delight.

I noticed June's stomach growing larger. Her face was full, and her temper frequently flared. It seemed the bigger she got, the meaner she was. I heard someone say, "She was in the family way." Even at twelve years old, I wasn't exactly sure what that meant, but I strongly suspected it meant she was going to have a baby.

I wondered how on earth the baby got inside June and how it was going to come out. I wouldn't dare ask anyone, not even my best friend. Private and delicate matters like this were never discussed among children. To inquire would be considered crude or brash. Adults allowed knowledge about such things to come later. I quelled my curiosity and merrily carried on about my life.

It wasn't much longer before Dr. Cotton was summoned. After many hours of labor, June's baby was finally born. Mama took June some chicken soup and hot cornbread muffins. In a few days, I brought my present for the baby - a little hat and booties that I had proudly crocheted. Little Mary was beautiful and tiny. I had never seen a baby so little and so red. She had a funny little cry, almost a whimper. She didn't look very strong, and secretly I was worried. June looked exhausted and had deep rings around her eyes. She sat up in bed with pillows puffed up around her. Mama said June must stay in bed for at least three weeks as that was the normal and proper thing for ladies to do after giving birth. June looked to me like she needed to stay in bed a long time. I still wasn't sure how that baby had come out, but it sure had left June looking a wreck. I surely didn't want any part of this ever!

Mr. Otjen began to worry about little Mary. She failed to gain weight and always seemed fretful. At six weeks old, she was taken to Oklahoma City to be examined by a specialist. The diagnosis was that she had a bad heart and "seizures." That is what happened when she trembled so. Our spirits sank and especially June's. June became subdued and withdrawn. She wasn't even mean - just quiet and sad. Pangs of compassion welled up in me as I thought about the plight of June and her fragile baby. I decided that I would help more, provide comfort, and hopefully see her smile again.

Things seemed to improve. Little Mary was growing slowly, and she was so pretty with her big blue eyes and blonde curly hair. She would clap her hands together and laugh out loud. June and Mr. Otjen were encouraged, and a measure of laughter and joy returned to their home. Smiles blossomed again. But the baby still had seizures. They were infrequent, yet always jolting us back into the reality that little Mary was a sick baby.

Chapter Twenty-Four-   *Looking Forward to the Mountains*

The seasons in Enid came and passed quickly. It was springtime again, and Mary was almost two years old. Her heart was still weak, and her periodic seizures continued.

Mr. Otjen had decided to build a house for June and little Mary in Manitou Springs, Colorado. There they could spend summers in the cool mountain air near the mineral baths. The mineral baths were said to cure many aliments and would hopefully reduce Mary's seizures. It would also help June's rheumatism that had developed.

I was pleasantly surprised when June invited me to spend the whole month of July and part of August in Colorado with her, Mr. Otjen, and Mary. As summer approached, I was thrilled. I had never seen the mountains before. We were to travel by train, and I pictured in my mind first seeing the mighty peaks of Colorado. How beautiful and majestic they must be!

The melody of summer soon filled the air. The crickets were chirping, and the roses were blossoming. The sounds of nature lingered in the breeze. Gentle echoes of children playing games in the distance could be heard. I watched the lace curtains blowing back and forth across my windowpane. It was all so peaceful. I just wanted to be still and to absorb it - memories of another Oklahoma summer to treasure forever.

As the time for the Colorado trip approached, I noticed June's stomach was growing large again. She was having headaches and crying spells symptomatically emerged. I prayed this baby would be strong, healthy, and a boy. No other little girl could take the place of little Mary in my heart.

Chapter Twenty-Five - Let's Light Up The World

It was early July, and we were finally on the train to Colorado. I was anxious to get there but also eager to view the countryside along the way. Little Mary was a bit fussy and confused by her new surroundings. June was uncomfortable and complaining. She dramatically lamented that she might die before we arrived. Mr. Otjen, who was usually sweet natured, seemed disgruntled. I decided to reserve my good humor and just enjoy the scenery along the way.

Today was Independence Day, and I had not anticipated any special celebration since this trip was celebration enough. I fixed my eyes through the window of our train berth to view the distant scenery. The sky above the high plains lit up in purple and red. The silhouettes of grazing cattle passed by us. Day would soon turn to night. These early evening impressions lingered in my mind. The rocking of the train upon the tracks made me drowsy.

Dozing off, I felt Mr. Otjen nudge my shoulder. I glanced warily around, and I saw his smile. June and little Mary were fast asleep. As I slowly rose from my seat, Mr. Otjen's eyes twinkled as he held a sack for me to open. Inside were bundles of Chinese fireworks. Mr. Otjen had not forgotten Independence Day! He motioned for me to follow. We wobbled to the back of the train, bumping walls along the way, as the train rumbled beneath us. Finally, Mr. Otjen swung open the last door. The rush of cool night air whooshed across my face. Standing side by side on the platform, we looked at each other and laughed. Lighting fireworks from a train seemed so delightfully absurd.

The first fireworks hit the tracks and were fast behind us as the red and blue sparks faded in the distance. We shot off a firecracker for Mary and sent it up as a prayer to God to renew her health. The second shot up was a rocket that poured red and gold sparks cascading over the sides of the invisible sky. As it disappeared into the night, I wished for a wonderful time in the mountains.

We lit the rest of the fireworks. The loud bangs, pops and sparks brought laughter and awe. Our celebration drew a little crowd on the train platform. Now we were all laughing and festive. Someone started singing the "Star Spangled Banner." We all joined in a rusty off-key chorus.

As everyone shuffled back inside the train, I told Mr. Otjen I would be quite alright outside for a while. He gave me his trusting look and turned to go inside. How I loved the stars. They shone like diamonds. It was as if I was looking into the eyes of God tonight. My heart raced with excitement, and I embraced the vibrancy of life all around me. I went back inside and fell fast asleep.

The train's wheels screeched as we arrived in Colorado Springs. The weary morning travelers stumbled down the stairs carrying their heavy luggage. We climbed into a taxi and took off to the mountains. Soon we arrived at Manitou Springs, a small mountain community that had been settled 30 years earlier as a health resort. This was to be my summer paradise for the next six weeks.

Chapter Twenty-Six - *Journey to Spacious Skies*

We arrived at our rental cottage nestled at the foot of the Rockies. The mountains behind the cottage majestically rose to the sky. The distant snowcaps reminded me of Christmas in summertime. The scent of fresh pine infused the cool brisk air. We had prayed that this fresh mountain air would strengthen Mary and revive June during the final months of her pregnancy.

I rushed up the stairs to peek into the cottage. It was appointed with simple furnishings, pink gingham curtains, and a coal oven for heat. June also looked in and seemed pleased.   Little Mary slept in her mother's arms unaware of her new surroundings. Mr. Otjen slowly climbed the stairs behind us lugging two large bags. As soon as he stepped inside the cottage, he dropped the bags and wearily slumped into the couch.   Mary whimpered as June plopped down beside Mr. Otjen. As much as I wanted to run outside and to enjoy these beautiful surroundings, I could see June and Mr. Otjen were fatigued.   I took the baby to change her diaper and to rock her for a while.

After unpacking and settling in, I stole a few moments in the afternoon to slip out the cottage door. The sun was warm upon my face. I ran down the pathway to the street below. People downtown were walking, riding on horseback, and driving automobiles. The homes stood grand and stately like overgrown gingerbread cottages lining the street. It was all very intriguing. Manitou Springs was a very wealthy community.

June's high-pitched voice was soon calling me back. I turned around and sprinted up the path. Little Mary had launched into one of her seizures. The seizure was over now, and she remained still and limp. The town doctor was summoned. He expressed concern and prescribed medication for June to administer to Mary. The doctor also examined June and prescribed for her lots of rest and mineral baths to heal her aching joints. From the events of the day, I realized much of my time in the mountains would be devoted to helping June and caring for Mary. But I still relished the thought of the few quiet moments I might have to myself in this special place. I snuggled down into my covers. The cool mountain air became cold, and I wrapped my shawl tighter around me as I drifted off to sleep.

The next morning, Mr. Otjen walked with June hand in hand to the mineral baths. I was left alone with Mary, who was a sweet but sickly toddler. I fed her mashed potatoes and milk - her favorites. We played "patty-cake," and Mary laughed and clapped before settling down for her nap. I curled up on the couch with my *Little Colonel* books waiting for June and Mr. Otjen to reappear.

June returned relaxed and content. Mr. Otjen seemed to be in better spirits. When Mary awoke, I took her for a stroll outdoors. It was a glorious green summer day. We became enthralled watching the Monarch butterflies hover above the mountain flowers. The mountain air turned Mary's cheeks rosy. She seemed to be growing stronger, and I hoped with all my might that she might be cured of all her ailments. When we returned to the cottage, Mr. Otjen had brought us ice cream. It tasted so cold and sweet. Mary gobbled her share and then drifted off to sleep.

Early the next day, Mr. Otjen woke me and said, "Get up Janey, we're going on a mountain hike." After he left the room, I drug myself out of bed and dressed for what I thought would be an early morning hike. We ate a hearty breakfast of eggs, ham, biscuits and juice. My stomach was so full that I wondered how I would make it up the mountain. After we finished eating, I asked, "Where are we going?" Mr. Otjen cocked his head and grinned as the summer wind tousled his dark hair. He gleefully declared, "We are going to climb to the summit of the master of mountains! To the top of Pikes Peak, we will climb!"

His enthusiasm was contagious. We carefully packed sleeping bags, warm clothes and other provisions in anticipation of an overnight adventure. Mr. Otjen soon bounced out the door with gusto. I hurried to keep up with him. With great determination, we marched down the cottage stairs to conquer the "King of Mountains." Knowing we would be gone for a day, Mr. Otjen had arranged for a woman from Manitou Springs to come and help care for June and Mary.

We chose the trail that was parallel to the trolley track that went up the mountain. It was clear of rocks and brush and was easier on the legs. Each time a trolley passed, the conductor and the passengers smiled and waved. After an hour or so, the trolley started up the mountain again. The conductor lifted his megaphone and announced to the passengers in a loud and amused voice, "Notice the two mountain goats on the right." Mr. Otjen and I quickly glanced to our right and then to our left. The joke was on us. We were the "mountain goats." The conductor loudly chuckled, and Mr. Otjen and I enjoyed a hearty laugh between ourselves. I turned and let out a loud "baah" as we continued up the mountain.

We stopped for lunch. I was amazed at all the mountain wildlife. Curious chipmunks scampered over the rocks around us. Stopping and staring at us, they appeared to beg for our crumbs. Two deer, a mother and a fawn, were nibbling on the meadow grass. They lifted their heads and looked at us as well. As much as I enjoyed these wonderful creatures, I was terrified of coming against a bear along the path. However, I didn't share this fear with Mr. Otjen lest he conclude I was not up to the adventure.

After lunch, we started again. The atmosphere was so fresh and alive. It gave me extra energy for our long ascent up the mountain. I knew we were making progress when I became light-headed and dizzy. The increasing elevation made breathing more difficult. Our breaks grew more frequent, and I began to lose motivation. Mr. Otjen encouraged me by saying we didn't have far to go. Twilight was falling on the mountain and soon it would be dark. An eerie feeling gripped me as I saw the sun set over the distant mountain range. I think Mr. Otjen shared the same feeling too. We became much more motivated to complete our climb as the daylight faded and the temperature plummeted. We removed our coats from our packs and wrapped them tightly around us. About an hour after sundown, we reached the summit. There would be no trolley until morning.

The moon soon shone full, and we could see the distant streetlights of Colorado Springs below and the silhouettes of the great hills. We had climbed 13 miles and it had taken nearly 10 hours. Surely, we were on top of the world. The sounds of night propelled upward to us in the deep quiet. I was simultaneously exhilarated and exhausted to the core of my being. My legs ached and trembled. I wearily rolled out my sleeping bag, climbed in, and fell fast asleep - pausing until morning the glory of the surrounding splendor.

The dawn came with rays of red, orange, and deep purple cast upon the sky. God must have been an artist. Never had I seen such glory in nature as I rubbed my sleepy eyes that July morning. I kicked back the bulk of my sleeping bag and rose to my feet. As I stood stiff and clumsy, I felt proud of our ascent to the mountain top. Mr. Otjen looked at me and nodded his head in approval for a mission well done. I shouted to the top of my voice, "We made it to the top, to the top of the Master Mountain!" My voice rolled down the mountain and echoed off the hills below. We sat silently enjoying the cool morning mist and breeze. We were too tired to move and each absorbed in our own thoughts of the mighty mountains around us. As a fourteen-year-old girl, I couldn't imagine that life could bring any greater thrill than this.

We waited for the trolley. When the sun had risen into full light, we could hear the rumbling of the engine churning up the mountainside. At last, as a long familiar friend, I caught sight of the red trolley coming to rescue our aching bones. The conductor laughed when he saw us, "Looks like you two mountain goats lost your luster." Mr. Otjen grinned half heartily and said, "The little lady's legs have just about given out. Do you think you might give us a ride to the bottom?" I had not complained of my legs. I thought Mr. Otjen must have great compassion until I spied him limping slowly to the trolley door. "A man's pride," I whispered under my breath. Mr. Otjen was too tired to hear my comment as we descended the mountain in luxury.

Rest was foremost on my mind. I knew Mr. Otjen and I must have been a sight to behold. Sweaty, exhausted, and hair unkempt, I recognized I had no chance of winning a prize that morning at any local beauty pageant. I just wanted to climb into bed and sleep for three days. In a daze, we clambered through the cottage door. June was up and scowling, Mary was crying for lunch. I quickly relinquished my plans for sleep and began helping to care for Mary.

Mary settled down and wanted a nap after lunch. I never thought I would be so excited to sleep. I sank into my feather bed and soon fell unconscious into a deep sleep. In a few days, Mama and Papa would be coming to visit. June and Mr. Otjen were anxious to show them the newly purchased land on which they planned to build their summer house. I was looking forward to seeing my parents. It had been more than a week since I left home, and I had so much to tell them.

Chapter Twenty-Seven - An Unplanned Drive

The home site was a picturesque mountainside property with a small level clearing perfectly suited for a house. A long and steep driveway meandered from the road below. There were no buildings except for an old barn in disrepair. The view was spectacular, overlooking great red rocks on one side and looking up at Pikes Peak on the other. One portion of the property bordered a steep cliff. Mr. Otjen and June had already decided to build a secure fence along that edge.

After an arduous three-day drive from Enid, Mama and Papa finally arrived. We all crammed into Papa's car to go see the new property. Mama and Papa were amazed at the beautiful spot where Mr. Otjen and June had chosen to build their home. June was explaining to Mama exactly where the house would be located. Absorbed in these details, we had forgotten about Mary. June stopped and cried, "Where's Mary?" She looked at me, and I turned to go find her. My heart screamed with terror.

The driver's side door to Papa's Model T Ford had been left open, and little Mary had climbed in. Playing with the levers, she had somehow mobilized the vehicle and it was now rolling slowly toward the cliff. My legs raced faster than my mind as I caught up with the car. I jumped into the driver's seat and shoved Mary aside. I had never been in control of a car before. Not having time to think, I knew enough that the steering wheel had something to do with the direction of the car. I pulled the wheel with all my might to one side and prayed with all my soul. As I held my breath in anticipation of disaster, the surrounding world seemed to spin in slow motion.

Mary's laughter turned to a stunned silence as we crashed into the barn. The splintering of wood exploded as the car went through the back of the barn. We were jolted forward against the front dash but somehow miraculously spared from serious injuries. I became dizzy and my stomach could not contain itself any longer. I vomited all over my dress. I turned and looked at Mary. Though pale and quiet, she sat alert and unharmed upon the seat. I was so relieved we were alive and grateful to the good Lord for saving our lives.

Mama, Papa, June and Mr. Otjen soon arrived at the scene with ghostly wide-eyed expressions on their faces. They were instantly relieved to see we were unharmed. June ran to the side of the car and grabbed Mary and drew her close. Mary sensed her panic and began to scream. Tears welled up in my eyes. I shuddered thinking about this nearly fatal accident from which Mary and I had been spared. Like a small child, I collapsed into my own Mama's arms and hugged her tightly. I could feel her trembling when she took me in her arms.

The car was dented a bit, but still operated fine. Papa drove us back to the cottage. We were reeling in shock and mostly silent. My parents were staying at the Cliff House Hotel in Manitou Springs. It was an enchanting place that reminded me of a castle next to a mountain. I went back to the hotel with Mama and Papa as I had a deep need to be near them. Secure in their presence, I slept.

When I awoke, I first thought the memory of the automobile heading for the cliff had only been a nightmare. But then I remembered it was all too real. We returned to June's for dinner that evening. I was sure no one felt quite up to it. As expected, June was at her worst. She snarled and snapped at Mr. Otjen for having left Mary unattended. However, I secretly suspected she blamed me for the whole ordeal. Yet, her strange stare at me that evening signaled a desperate sense of gratitude. It was hard to interpret what she was thinking.

We didn't stay long. As we drove back to the hotel, Papa held my hand and told me how proud he was of me. He said that not many girls would have had the courage or the quickness of mind to act as fast as I had. He said, "You're a fine girl, Janey! An exceptionally fine person." I was grateful someone was giving me due recognition for my heroic act. Even June and Mr. Otjen, once calmed about the ordeal, expressed their great appreciation for what I had done. However, in my heart, I knew it had been the hand of God that saved us.

The rest of the month was spent caring for Mary and taking her on long walks in the sunshine, picnicking by the creek, and growing to love her more. It had been a wonderful summer in the mountains, but I was anxious to go home to my own house, my own room, and my good friends.

Chapter Twenty-Eight - Leaving Colorado for Home

As the end of August approached, the days and evenings in Manitou Springs grew a bit cooler, and I knew it was time to leave. June and Mr. Otjen had plans to take Mary to Chicago where a well-known doctor had said he could help. However, June first had to go back to Enid to have her baby and to wait out the proper recovery time. Mr. Otjen, June and little Mary returned to Enid by train. We were concerned about June and Mary as they both appeared weak and exhausted.

I rode back with Mama and Papa in the Model T Ford. The driving distance from Manitou Springs to Enid was over 500 miles. Once we came down out of the mountains, it was a long, hot, and windy ride. We stopped the first night just across the Kansas border and felt better after a bath and a good meal. It was difficult to climb back into the automobile for another endless day. As we rumbled and tossed over the dirt roads, we were tired and eager to get home. On the third day, we finally drove into Enid at dusk each quietly rejoicing at the sight of our house.

The end of August in Enid was brutal as the air was hot and dusty. There was no relief from the heat. How different from the Colorado mountains where we had been just a few days before. We put on our bathing clothes and went to the lake. But even there the water was stale and tepid. At night I sat on the front porch and ate fruit with Mama and Papa as we prayed for rain. We just wanted something to bring relief from the heat. Gazing up into the bright night sky, I would count the shooting stars and sing to myself.

Summer would soon be over, and school would begin. I would be entering high school at the age of 14. The lazy, hazy days of a long summer would soon dissolve into the cooler, rainy days of autumn. Mama was busy sewing my dresses for school. I would have three new ones this year. Though not as tall as my sisters, I was growing fast.

June was preparing for her new baby. She was crocheting new gowns and sewing soft blankets. She was tired and pale. Mary was still stricken by seizures. Although we had all learned to deal with them, they were a constant reminder of how extremely ill she was.

Chapter Twenty-Nine - Where Angels Live

It was late September. June was distraught by Mary's continued seizures, and now Mary's facial color grew much worse. Her lips had turned blue. Mr. Otjen and June hurriedly made arrangements to take Mary by train to Chicago so she could be treated by Dr. Dawson. He was a well- respected heart surgeon who thought he might be able to correct Mary's condition. It would require surgery. This posed a risk to Mary's life, but without it she would surely perish.

June and Mr. Otjen were fearful but hopeful as they boarded the train in with their precious Mary. Their new baby boy, William, would have to be left behind in Mama's care. Thankfully, William, who had been born just a few weeks before, was perfectly healthy. I reached out to give Mary a gentle hug. Mary's eyes were big and round, and she trembled so. I didn't want this dear little child to sense the deep fear I had for her inside of me. Handing her a handkerchief that I had tatted an edging on, I told her it was hers to keep. She smiled in her sweet angelic way and took it from my hand. "Bye, bye, Janey," she waved. My throat grew tight and tears welled up in my eyes. I tried to smile as I replied, "Bye bye, I'll miss you my Angel." I glanced away quickly so nobody would see the tears that were flowing down my face. Mama turned and gently reprimanded me, "Don't Janey, don't."

I knew Mama was right. We had to be strong. We had to think the best. We had to pray and have faith. I managed to contain myself as we walked away in silence. Mary's pretty baby face lingered in my mind, so innocent. She was my first niece. So many special moments had been spent with her in Colorado and in Enid while June was convalescing. In many ways, I felt as if Mary was my child too. I knew Jesus realized how important she was to each of us. I was so hopeful he would not take her from us. I wanted to believe that with all my heart, but a gnawing fear continued to grow.

The surgery was scheduled for two days after their arrival in Chicago. June and Mr. Otjen would telegram us about the outcome as soon as possible. We attended church and prayed extra prayers. All of us were a bundle of nerves. On the day of surgery, the family gathered in the living room. Mama and I knelt and cried out to God on Mary's behalf. Papa came and joined us and soon Douglas did too. We were joined in a common and desperate plea for Mary's life. I pled especially hard. I would do anything to have Mary live - even become a missionary in a far-off land. She had to live. I couldn't stand it if she didn't. The minutes seemed like hours. Time was a prison that would not free me until the sentence on Mary's life was lifted.

The room turned hazy as the late afternoon sun beamed through the window. There was a knock on the front door. Suddenly I dreaded the message that might be coming. Please don't let the telegram man be here, I thought to myself. I would rather remain in time's prison than to be exposed to devastating news. Papa slowly read the telegram from Mr. Otjen out loud, "Mary died at 3:15 p.m. She went to be with Jesus. Home tomorrow on the 6:00 o'clock train." Mama wailed, clutching her apron, and reliving all the despair of her own loss of a child that she had experienced more than 20 years before. Papa crumbled the telegram in his hand and stumbled out of the room with his head hanging low. Douglas and I stared at each other reeling in shock and disbelief over what we had just heard.

As Douglas moved toward me, I bolted from the house. I had to be alone. I couldn't deal with something for which I was at such a loss to understand. I fled toward the wheat fields, running faster and harder, as my heart was breaking. When I could run no longer, I collapsed into the red clay soil and screamed, tormented Mary had died. It was dark when I returned. My dress was stained with soil. My hair was caked in mud, and no one seemed to notice when I walked in. I mournfully shuffled upstairs to bathe. My family sat in the dark living room in silence. Only a few muffled sobs rose in the night.

There was a slight tapping at the back door. I rose to go see who it was. It was Glen Johnston. I didn't want to see him. He said, "Your niece, Mary? Did she come through the surgery alright?" I opened the back door and stepped down. I looked at Glen and stated coldly, "Mary died at 3:15 this afternoon." His eyes filled with compassion. It was more than I could bear. "Oh, Janey, I am so sorry." Before I knew what was happening, emotion overwhelmed me, and I collapsed into his arms and wept. I don't know how long I was there, but I stumbled back into the house in a daze and fell asleep, too tired to care.

In the morning, Mama came into my room. She gently patted my head and spoke softly, "Janey, honey, I know how difficult this is for you, you loved Mary so, but we must think of June today." I realized Mama was right. June would be coming home with the lifeless body of her child.

I knew that we had to be strong for her and walk her through these dark days. After pausing, Mama added, "We have to do this Janey! Please deal with your feelings in private but not in June's presence."

Mr. Otjen and June arrived later that day as scheduled. Mr. Otjen did not look up as his head was bent in grief. June was visibly shaken. We helped them from the train and drove them home. Their house was clean and full of food. It did not matter. June went straight to bed. Mary's funeral was tomorrow.

In the morning, Mama and I went early to June's house to assist her. She was silent and pale. We helped help her dress, fix her hair, and lace her shoes. June stared blankly. Then she wailed, "My baby died," She paused and wailed even louder, "My baby died." Mama held her, and June sobbed. I sobbed too because of June's agony and because of my own pain for the loss of Mary.

The whole town showed up. The tiny casket lay before us. I knew Mary was with Jesus and not in the casket. I still wanted her with us here on earth. I did not want Jesus to whisk her away to heaven. The minister's words flew over my head. I didn't even try to comprehend a word he said. I was relieved when the funeral ended so I could go home and endure my suffering in solitude.

Maybe Jesus would heal our hearts. Feeling numb and nauseous, I just wanted to sleep. That I did, and we all did. Maybe it was a healing sleep. As the days passed, it became a little easier to wake up each morning absorbing the reminder of Mary's death. June had dark days, but her new baby was so precious and renewed her spirits. And she would have more healthy children. They were the grace that allowed her to live and overcome her grief.

But we knew Mary would always be June's first child. Nothing would change that truth. Nothing would take away the special place we held for her in our hearts. We would always miss her and feel the void left by her absence on earth. Yet, we were also greatly comforted knowing that we would surely see her again in heaven.

Chapter Thirty - Those Wonderful High School Days

Another year passed and it was September once again. Enid continued to grow as oil production boomed. Mr. Otjen's law practice prospered as June delighted in her two new children. Douglas had gone off to college. Papa's reputation as a fair and thoughtful judge increased across the State. In a few more years he would be elected to the Oklahoma Supreme Court. Mama quietly enjoyed all these gifts from God. At the age 15, I was no longer a little girl but a young woman.

Today I would be beginning my second year of high school. I could not decide on what outfit to wear. Mother had bought me a dainty midi-blouse which was gorgeous and thought I would wear it with my navy skirt. I hoped Glen Johnston would be seated near me. I remembered and cherished his compassionate embrace on that night Mary had died. I heard Glen was going to military school next semester, and I really wanted to get better acquainted before he left. Glen was shy and very handsome. He was tall with long features and dark hair and eyes. I knew he liked me. He always said hello, and I noticed him watching me when he thought I was unaware. I had never thought much about boys before. However, I thought about Glen a lot, and I hoped we would share some time together.

The school smelled of fresh paint. As I walked into my classroom, I pretended not to notice as I slipped into a desk across from Glen. I busily chattered with Betsy about upcoming social events. Chautauqua was coming to Enid next summer. It would be an exciting introduction to classical music and literature, ushering in culture to our little corner of the world. Musicians, actors, singers and poets would gather under one big canopy to entertain and educate us in the timeless delights of the arts. These festivities were to last five days around the lake, and the whole town was to be involved. When the teacher entered the room, we stood silently. I glanced at Glen, whose eyes were gazing upon me. I blushed with embarrassment. He seemed amused as we took our seats.

The school guild was new and so were our ideas. There was one that I wanted to launch into action. I believed that a school newspaper was just what we needed to inform students and teachers about community events. I proposed this idea, and I was thrilled when it was approved. We quickly chose our staff writers. I was elected secretary. What an honor to serve our school in this way! We all held our positions on the guild in highest regard.

There was also a fraternity and a sorority forming in our high school. Boys called their club the Sphinx. They rented a small clubhouse off the square, and the girls' sorority shared it. I was not impressed with the idea of a sorority. It excluded many girls, including me. The first year the sorority was established, the girls sat through lunch gossiping and laughing. We strongly suspected they were talking about the rest of us by the arrogant expressions on their faces. They sneered, giggled, and glanced our way. Wilma Lamar had just been accepted into the group. She was not rich, but extremely unique.

This whole idea of the sorority pained me more day after day. It weighed on my mind. Who did those girls think they were? They saw themselves as exquisite and better than the rest. I knew that I had many imperfections, but I was not exactly a "low man" on the totem pole. I couldn't understand why they excluded me and other friends. I would never treat another human being in such a degrading manner. I resented it greatly not only for myself but for all the other girls who were being excluded.

As the weeks passed, I relinquished some of my resentment toward the sorority girls, and my mind became occupied by other thoughts. The first school dance was approaching in a several weeks. It would be my first dance ever. Being a good Methodist, Papa did not approve of his daughters attending dances. But I had to find a way to attend despite Papa's feelings. This would be the most important event in my life up until now. I would surely die if I were forbidden to go.

Glen's older brother, Dale, was learning to dance. His mother was eager for him to learn all the proper social graces. I guess that is what prompted her to call my mother. She asked Mama if I could be Dale's dance partner. Mrs. Johnston was hiring a private dance instructor at her home. Dale was to be my partner. I was surprised she phoned but thrilled to be receiving private dance instructions. We would learn to waltz and fox-trot as well as all the new dances. I could not wait for my first dance lesson. I just hoped that Papa would not object.

I couldn't believe it! Downtown in front of the ice cream parlor stood Wilma Lamar. Usually refined in all her ways, Wilma was pacing on the corner with her dress on backwards selling pencils. How idiotic! You would not catch me doing that for a million dollars. I was beginning to have serious doubts about the girls of Alpha Sigma Tau. Maybe they were just fools instead of snobs.

Betsy and I ate our ice cream and stopped to greet Wilma in her silly state. She said, "Janey, go home now. You'll be getting a very important phone call this afternoon. You won't want to miss it!" A bit surprised, I replied, "I'm headed that way right now, Wilma." Betsy and I skipped home. It was no sooner that I had said good-bye to Betsy and burst through the front door when the telephone rang. "Hello," I answered. The female voice on the other end giggled and said, "Jeannette, guess what?" I still was not sure who it was. After a pause, the caller squealed in delight, "You have been voted into the Alpha Sigma Tau Sorority! Isn't that the best?" Smugly I replied, "Well I am going to have to think about it. And another thing, if I'm initiated, I will not sell pencils on the square, eat raw eggs or sit on chunks of ice!" After a moment of silence, the voice on the other end replied, "Well I never! We will have to bring this up with our council and get back in touch with you."

What a day! I sighed as I hung up and marched up to my room to take a short nap. Tonight, I was to have my first dancing lesson with Dale Johnston. Mrs. Johnston would pick me up at 6:00 p.m. It was 5:00 p.m. when I awoke. I barely had enough time to freshen up before Dale was at the door. I ran to kiss Mama and Papa good-bye, grabbed my sweater, and turned for the door. Mama had strongly appealed to Papa to allow me to take these lessons. He relented only because he knew how much this meant to me. As I walked out the door, I saw him looking at me with reluctant approval.

I felt very dignified riding in the Johnston's shiny new car to my first dance lesson. The lesson was conducted in the Johnston's living room. Our dance instructor was a tall and distinguished old gentleman. Dale was a superb dancer and learned fast. I felt like a princess dancing. We waltzed, fox-trotted, tangoed, and learned all the new dances. These lessons were to continue twice a week for the next four weeks. Returning home starry eyed and immersed in thoughts of romance, I drifted off to sleep. I dreamed that I was wearing a flowing dress, light as a feather, and softly dancing in a stranger's arms.

This was becoming a great year. I had been elected President of my junior class. My first dance was approaching, and I was excelling in school. I loved my German class, and I had joined the glee club and choral group. My friends were the best and the brightest. I only wished that those sorority girls would stop being such silly snobs. I believed there was so much more good that a sorority could do.

I was also thrilled that my brothers and sisters were doing well. Douglas was playing football at college. Irene was attending the Iowa Teachers College specializing in teaching kindergarten, a new course for the very young. May was teaching school in Dover, Oklahoma. Jimmy was carrying mail and working at the courthouse while he studied law.

June was enjoying motherhood, and her husband's law practice was thriving.

In late October, a big picnic was planned at Lakewood Park. We were all going to be there. The Cullisons, the Drummonds, the Champlins, the Stephensons, and the Johnstons. When the day of the picnic arrived, the weather was perfect. A gentle fall breeze swept through the park and the sun warmed us. The trees bent above the mirrored lake, and the wind gently rocked our swing. We played croquet on the lawn and sat on our blankets, dreaming of our futures with the ecstasy of youth.

On the Saturday following the picnic, the time for our school dance have finally arrived. Mama had bought me my first pair of dance shoes. They were beautiful pink ballet slippers that I carried in a fancy bag. Preparing for the dance, I recalled one of my mother's favorite sayings, "A little powder, a little paint makes a girl what she ain't," I quietly laughed as I thought tis true, tis true. My dress was beautiful. Mama had made it. It was navy taffeta adorned with lace trim and a very delicate tatting along the cuffs. I wore a huge white lace bow in my hair.

Examining myself in the mirror I questioned, was I pretty? I felt pretty. My long black hair was unique among my peers. My jaw was dominate and square, my eyes were large, round, and green. My lips were full, but not large. I stood 5 feet 4 inches tall and was small boned. I felt on top of the world. When I carefully dressed and primped, I felt beautiful. After one last glance of self-admiration, I was out the door.

Mrs. Johnston was parked out front in her fancy Cadillac waiting for me. Dale was handsome wearing his new blue suit. He opened the car door for me, and I daintily slid across the seat. I felt eloquent as we drove off to the dance. Dropping us off at the front of the school, Mrs. Johnston said she would return to pick us up.

As we entered the dance area, I was confident Dale and I would be among the best dancers there. I picked up my dance card. Immediately Jim Fluging, a boy who had just moved from Wichita, signed up for four dances on my card. Dale wrote his name in three more dances, and Lee Fields came by and wrote his name down for the last dance. My dance card was full. I was ecstatic. No wallflower I would be tonight!

Not long after the dance began, Betsy Drummond approached me and stammered "I suppose you've heard." "Heard what?" I inquired. Betsy explained that five of the sorority girls had vowed to drop out if I joined. They did not like my attitude and my reluctance to comply with their initiation rules. Out of curiosity I asked who the five girls were. It turned out they were the biggest snobs of all. "Come on, Janey" Betsy pled, "Can't you go along with it instead of igniting this whole sorority into uproar?" Betsy had been a member of Alpha Sigma Tau since it began. I quickly replied, "Not a chance." Betsy sneered a bit and turned away.

The rest of the time flew by that evening. I relished every minute. Every dance was enchanting. I most enjoyed dancing with Dale and showing off our talents. None of the other students had been taking dance lessons like us. The dance came to end before I knew it. It had been everything I had hoped it to be… absolutely splendid!

On Monday, following the dance, I was full of apprehension. The prospect of joining the Alpha Sigma Tau sorority still weighed on my mind. My desire was to join but only if the sorority was willing to become something much better than it was. As was their custom, some of the sorority girls sat together that day in the cafeteria, whispering, glaring, and giggling among themselves. If they were going to keep behaving like this, I did not want any part of it. Toward the end of the lunch period, the sorority president, Ruthie Jones, approached me and asked to speak to me after school. I agreed.

School ended quicker than I wanted that day. Ruthie met me in an empty classroom. After sitting down, she took a deep breath and said, "Jeannette, you were voted in twice. We really want you. We are willing to dissolve our initiation activities if you join." I was absolutely stunned as Ruthie continued, "Five of our members are quitting because they don't like change. But the rest of us know you will be great asset to our group." I was flabbergasted that this sorority wanted me enough to allow five of its members to quit. I smiled and said, "I will be very honored to accept your invitation but only if Alpha Sigma Tau will become open to all girls within our student body who want to join." Ruthie smiled, "You are not easy, Jeannette, but we have already talked about that and agree." I thanked her and affirmed, "I'll join."

I walked away with a sense of victory. I had stood up for what I knew was right. Instead of remaining a snobbish clique, our sorority would become a charitable organization open to all and committed to the achievement of women in our society. It would be more than just a club

– it would be a sisterhood reaching out to serve others and intent on making better tomorrows for our community. I was elected president the next year. We changed our name to AET's and our sorority became the positive organization that I had hoped it would be all along.

Chapter Thirty-Two - Chautauqua

It was now 1916. I had just finished my second year of high school. Enid was expanding quickly and had become one of the largest cities of Oklahoma. The recent discovery of the nearby Garber-Covington oil field had boosted our economy. Enid was also advancing in culture. We had a library, a new high school, and even a thriving college, Phillips University.

Chautauqua would soon be arriving and performing for five days. All events would be held at Lakewood Park. There would be an orchestra, Shakespearean plays, soloists and the famous poet, Byron, was to recite. These were events that both young and old could enjoy. We were all starved for culture.

Many families would bring tents to camp. A few summer homes were already built. No doubt a few well to do families would occupy those. Irene was to oversee childcare, and May would assist her. They would be staying at a house in the park. The joyful anticipation of this event spread like wildfire through the county. Talk of Chautauqua was everywhere

Today, I decided to go downtown to window shop for outfits that I might wear to Chautauqua. It was a warm and dusty day. Feeling a little blue and bored, I really did not care how I appeared. Dressed in the first clothes I could grab, I rode the streetcar to town. While gazing at the newest fashions in the window of Herzberg's Department Store, I saw the Johnston's Cadillac cruising up to the curb. Out stepped Mrs. Johnston, her brown-gray hair slicked back in a bun and appearing very dignified.

Glen accompanied her. He was in his military uniform, tall, thin, and extremely dashing. His wavy brown hair was combed to one side. His dreamy, brown eyes met mine, and I blushed and turned quickly. I looked so disheveled, but I will never forget the way he presented himself - so gallant and tall. I was love struck.

Glen was going to be working for his father this summer in the grain business. The Johnston family owned the grain business in Enid and in surrounding towns. Our families had shared in founding this new state together and participating in the Cherokee Strip Land Run. Mr. Johnston had a gentle manner. He always poured the extra seed into flour sacks to give the poor so they could plant small crops and harvest food to eat. Even if they had a little money, he would never ask for a dime. This was an admirable quality in a man. Despite his annoying antics as a younger boy, I knew Glen must have generosity flowing through his blood too.

The day of Chautauqua finally arrived. We brought blankets and parasols, paper, and pencil. We were in ecstatic anticipation of the upcoming events. The first program was the Shakespearean play, a scene from the Merchant of Venice. Mother and I sensed chills as we heard the Thespian recite, "The Quality of Mercy," and "earthly power doth then show like God's mercy seasons justice." When the Thespian ended the verse, a complete silence permeated the audience, followed by an outpouring of applause and cheers. We were all impressed by the authenticity of the Shakespearean costumes and the intricate details of the designs.

116

Scheduled next on the program was the orchestra playing Beethoven's Fifth Symphony. I closed my eyes as I listened to the music. The violins and the cellos were mystical. This was just the beginning of the week, and each night seemed better than the evening before. I was deeply inspired to practice my music with new fervor. I will never forget the thrill of those five summer nights with the whole town gathering for enjoyment. We became a bit gay, lighter and a touch friendlier. All of us were laying on blankets or sitting on chairs under the full moon listening to the orchestra while stars danced and the whole universe seemed copasetic. Even grouchy old Mrs. Nybergen had a glowing smile upon her face.

Chautauqua felt magical! There was, however, one embarrassing moment. Mr. Peabody was scheduled to play the piano. He was brilliant and his reputation for being an excellent musician preceded him. Mr. Newcastle was slated to introduce him. Mr. Newcastle had an aversion to public speaking. Yet, due to the pressure of his peers, he reluctantly agreed to introduce this famous pianist. The room was filled to capacity. A hush fell on the crowd, and Mr. Newcastle appeared boldly announcing: "Now Mr. Playbody will pee a tune for you!" I don't think I have ever seen anybody turn so red as Mr. Newcastle who fled the room. Mr. Peabody immediately began to play, and I bit my cheek so hard to keep from laughing that it bled. I could hear a lot of coughing behind me. Folks all over the room were trying as hard as they could to keep from laughing. This would surely be recorded in my personal annals as one of the funniest memories of my early life. However, being sensitive to Mr. Newcastle's humiliating faux pas, my mother turned to me with a grin and said, "We shall never refer to it again."

Sunday morning arrived too quickly as usual. I struggled to overcome my sleepiness as I slipped into my church clothes. Mama was putting old clothes I had outgrown in a box so they could be delivered to missionaries. After church, the deacons were coming for dinner. Oh, pain. I knew it was for Mama too, as everything and everyone had to be nearly perfect. Papa was dressed in his derby hat and black suit looking like his distinguished self. As I rambled down the stairs, I heard Mama yelling "Hurry Jeannette or we'll be late!" "I am coming! I am coming," I exclaimed, as I plodded along. I was dreading another long sermon, yet I loved to sing the hymns. They were heaven's music, and I drew close to Jesus when I sang them.

I snapped out of my dreariness when I realized Glen was sitting one row behind me, I was anxious to speak to him, yet reluctant, too. What if I something stupid escaped my mouth? I did not trust what would roll from my tongue in my state of nervousness. When church was over, Glen approached and extended a greeting, "Hello, Jeannette." He grinned in a mild-mannered way, half embarrassed. He was shy and reserved, the qualities that melted my heart. Glen inquired if he could come over to visit me that evening. I replied that I would be completely delighted, and I was.

The "after church" dinner was a drawn-out affair. The deacons rambled on about the missionaries, church ethics, and lots of other boring things. I could tell Papa was growing weary too. Papa livened the conversation by offering to tell one of his favorite courtroom stories. Mama seemed a bit squeamish, but Papa proceeded to tell his tale:

119

Two years ago, I presided over a case in Garfield County where a bootlegger by the name of Johnson was on trial. Johnson had been brewing moonshine whiskey in a still up in the hills, and the only eyewitness to the crime was an old man, Harless Jones who lived in the backwoods. He wore tattered clothes and an old dirty cap and was fondly known as 'Ole Hars' Ole Hars didn't like to talk to people, and he was very uncomfortable in a courtroom. The prosecuting attorney, Mr, Fletcher, began his questioning of Ole Hars. 'Now Hars,' he began, 'Did you see Mr. Johnson cut across the creek, hike through the berry patch, go over Smith's fence and head up the patch into the woods?' Hars hesitated and Mr. Fletcher became adamant, 'Hars, did you see him?' 'Mmmm, yes sir, I believe I did,' finally came the reply. Mr. Fletcher pushed his questioning, 'Well what did you think when you saw Mr. Johnson cut across the creek, hike through the berry patch, go over Smith's fence, and head up the path into the woods?' Hars hesitated and responded slowly 'I don't really recall.' 'Hars,' Mr. Fletcher pleaded, 'I repeat, what did you think when you saw Mr. Johnson cut across the creek, hike through the berry patch, go over Smith's fence, and head up the path into the woods? Hars. what did you say to yourself when you saw this?' Hars paused and thought awhile and finally blurted out: 'Well, I said to myself, there goes Mister Johnson.'

Papa heartily laughed as he concluded this story, and we laughed too. No matter how many times Papa told this story we always laughed. Even the stodgy deacons laughed, and our long lunch ended on a lighter note.

When the deacons left, I told Mama that Glen was coming to visit. With a twinkle in her eye, Mama announced she would make lemonade for us. "Thank you, Mama," I exclaimed as I rushed off to freshen up. Glenn arrived, and he was wearing his uniform again. I hoped Papa would be impressed as I knew Papa had a great respect for the military and soldiers. However, Papa wasn't pleased to see Glen at all. For some unknown reason, he shook his head and excused himself immediately. Glen and I breezed out to the porch swing. We drank lemonade and chatted quietly. I was extremely self-conscious when I was in Glen's presence. While we were talking on the porch, the telephone rang. It was Mrs. Johnston. She invited me to come and teach Glen to dance. I was thrilled and eagerly accepted.

Accompanied by a pianist, the same distinguished dance instructor who taught me and Dale returned to teach Glen and me. Glen turned out to be a better dancer than Dale. We spent many hours together that summer drinking lemonade, chatting and feeling giddy. Glen was so innocent, shy, and charming, and I was very drawn to him. He was enrolled at Kemper Military Academy in Boonville, Missouri, and I dreaded that autumn when he would vanish again until the holidays.

Chapter Thirty-Four - Seventeen

The seasons passed. Glen had gone back to the military academy in Missouri and had just returned again for summer. Today, I was graduating from "Old Enid High." In another week, I would turn seventeen years old. It was hard to believe that time had passed so quickly. At last, I would be "out on my own!" What does that mean? I did not want to go to college and become a teacher like my sisters. I would prefer to work at the courthouse with Papa, but I knew he would never allow me to be a secretary. He told me once that worldly girls were secretaries, and he would rather die than have one of his daughters work for a man in an office.

I decided not to think about my future right now. Rather, I would think about the dance tonight and my beautiful red, off-the shoulder dress with puffed sleeves and taffeta ruffles which fell all the way to the floor. Tonight, I would be with Glen Johnston. I was excited he had finally returned to Enid after what seemed a long time. The Judge knew I was going to the graduation dance, and he was not pleased. Although he ruled his courtroom with great authority, he did not always have the final say in his own home.   In this instance, he had deferred to the persuasive pleas of his wife and the emotional fancies of his daughter.

As I walked up the steps to receive my diploma, a flood of emotions overcame me. I was proud to be living in Enid.   I was proud that Oklahoma had been a state for 10 years. I wondered if my friends whom I held so dear would drift away. I wondered if I would ever see them again. I wondered if I would ever be as happy as I was today or if life would become difficult from now on. As I was handed my diploma, I looked out and saw Papa and Mama beaming with pride.

When Glen knocked on our door that evening, Mama let him in. I waited at the top of the stairs. Slowly and deliberately I descended each step with the utmost grace until I stood in front of Glen's handsome face. I had loved him since I was fourteen years old. At that moment, I knew he had always loved me. He had loved me even when he put my pigtails in the ink well and when he stepped on my feet in dance class. He loved me when I cried on his shoulder when Mary died. He was my friend. He had never gone out with any other girl but me. I was his true love, and he was mine!

We danced and danced that evening. We seemed all alone in each other's arms. The band played, "I love you as I never loved before, when you are sweet sixteen." Too soon, the dance was over. Glen drove me to Betsy Drummond's house for the slumber party. We pulled up in front of the house, he leaned over and kissed me. He looked at me with a gleam in his eyes and said, "Let's drive to Perry in the morning and get married! I will pick you up at nine o'clock." Without hesitation, I enthusiastically answered, "Yes."

Be married! This is exactly what I wanted to do! There was no reason to wait. This way we would always be together. As I snuggled down in bed, I tugged the covers to myself and tried to fall asleep -- but not before I told Betsy my secret. She swore on the Bible that she would not tell a living soul. It was a sleepless night. I knew this decision was extremely impulsive. Beyond our hastily planned trip to Perry, Glen and

I had not thought out any details about our new life together. But, oh well, I was committed now! At 9:00 a.m. sharp, Glen arrived as promised. Strutting confidently up the sidewalk, he wore his military uniform. My eyes transfixed on his handsome face. Giddiness overcame me. In just a few hours, he would be all mine! My husband! I would be Mrs. Glen Johnston.

We arrived in Perry, the county seat of Noble County about 40 miles east of Enid. We lied about our age. The judge at the courthouse believed Glen when he said he was home from the war and had to return to base in three days. That was the summer of 1917, and American soldiers were fighting fiercely in France under the command of General John Pershing. I remained calm. I had spent so much time with my father at the courthouse that I felt completely home in the judges' chambers. Then, as the marriage ceremony began, I was suddenly shaking with nervousness. The exchange of vows was brief. I did not even realize what the judge was saying until I heard, "I now pronounce you man and wife." Glen kissed me and said, "I love you, Janey." I knew at that moment I could never love anyone else like I loved Glen Johnston.

As we walked out of the courthouse, hand in hand, we walked smack dab into Aunt Daisy. She was Glen's aunt and was very peculiar. Aunt Daisy wore old hats that she stored for years in her closet. Every now and then, you might see a moth fly out of one of the flowers mounted on her hat. As to why she was in Perry that morning, we had no idea. "What are you two doing?" she sternly asked and raised an eyebrow in suspicion. I quickly concocted an explanation and replied, "Oh I just came to the courthouse to check on a case for my father." Although clearly suspicious, she refrained from asking any more probing questions and walked away.

We returned to Enid. Our elation soon subsided as we faced the reality that we were married and had no plan for what would happen next. We became worried. We did not want anyone to learn about our marriage until we had broken the news to our parents. And we still had no idea how we were going to do that. I decided I would go back to Betsy's slumber party. Glen said he would change clothes and go back to work. That night we would be together again and contrive how we were going to break the news to our parents.

Two weeks passed. Each night, Glen and I had sat on my porch swing and plotted how we would announce our marriage. No good plan emerged that could overcome the shock that we knew this would cause. On this day, Glen called to tell me that I was invited to his house for dinner. Maybe they knew. Did Aunt Daisy spill the beans? Did Betsy tell someone? I was nervous.

When I arrived at the Johnston house, Mrs. Johnston was in the kitchen carving quail for dinner. The Johnstons frequently served wild game as they were avid hunters. I could not bring myself to eat anything with feathers. Mother would pick the feathers off a chicken when it was dead, and I could not stand to look at a chicken, much less eat it.

We sat down at the table to eat. When Mrs. Johnston passed the quail to me, I said, "I am sorry, but I am not very hungry." She inquired if I liked quail, "No, I replied." "How strange," she answered. Mr.

Johnston just sat quietly staring at us with a peculiar expression. Glen became extremely uncomfortable and began to squirm. Mr. Johnston turned and looked straight at Glen and said, "We heard a rumor that you and Janey ran off and got hitched two weeks ago." Glen replied truthfully, "Yes sir, we did." There was dead silence. Everyone at the table turned to see what Mr. Johnston would say next.

After what seemed like an eternity, Mr. Johnston smiled his sweet smile that we all knew so well. He said, "That's wonderful news! Now we just have to decide what you two are going to do with your lives." Relief flooded the room. It was settled. Mr. Johnston had everything planned. We would move to the nearby town of Goltry, and Glen would operate the grain elevator business there. But we still needed to tell my parents.

The next morning, Glen and I walked to my house arm in arm. Douglas was standing near the house. Glen announced, "Douglas, I want you to meet my wife, Mrs. Glen Johnston." Douglas turned as white as a sheet, but he shook Glen's hand firmly and gave me a hug. "Does the Judge know?" he asked. I shook my head. With that, Douglas raced several blocks and burst into the courthouse. He bolted up to my father in the middle of a hearing and excitedly conveyed, "Papa, Janey is married!" "Who to?" Papa gruffly asked. "Young Johnston?" He had sternly and correctly answered his own question. Papa slammed down his gavel and said, "Court is adjourned!"

Meanwhile, I telephoned Mama in Dover, Oklahoma where she was helping May care for her new baby. I requested that she return home on the next train because I needed to tell her something of the utmost urgency. The train was to arrive that afternoon. June accompanied me to the station. I was certain the only reason she came was to see how badly Mama would react to this shocking news.

The train pulled into the station. A puff of steam shot from the engine. I rubbed my eyes and looked up. Mama was sprinting toward me. She grabbed me, "What is wrong, what is wrong?" June was standing right beside me when I answered, "Mama, I am married. I married Glen." Mama shook me and kept saying, "You are not! You are not!" I started to giggle. June, with a stern face, glared and said, "You won't be laughing ten years from now." These warnings could not dampen the excitement of the day. I was in love with Glen, and he was in love with me.

After our families had absorbed the initial shock, we set about to follow Mr. Johnston's plan. Goltry, Oklahoma was a small community about 25 miles northwest of Enid. The Johnstons owned a grain facility there. This is where we would make our new home and where Glen would work. Although I dearly loved Glen, the reality of leaving my family soon stuck a chord of sorrow. This would be my new life with my new husband.

At 17 years old, I was a young wife. I had lived a sheltered life and was still mostly ignorant about the "birds and the bees." The only practical advice my mother had given was "When they get to breathing heavy, send them home." Now, Mama had to explain sex to me before we left for Goltry. I was terrified.

Mama gathered as many household supplies as she could. With the help of my siblings, we packed as much as we could in the Model T Ford. The trunk was full of dishes, pots, and bedding. Some household goods would be shipped by train. Mama and Papa would drive us to Goltry.

Before climbing into the back seat of the car, I turned to look back at our house, and a thousand memories flooded my mind. Life would never be the same! As the drive began, an awkward silence filled the car that screamed my parent's disapproval. I glanced at my new husband, and he gently smiled back at me. I bowed my head and prayed a silent prayer as we drove on the dusty road from Enid.

EPILOGUE

After a short stint working in the grain industry, Jeannette and Glen left Oklahoma to purchase a cattle ranch in Delhart, Texas. They lived there for nearly 20 years and had 2 children, Willis and Jeanneane. Sadly, June's prediction came true. Over the years, Glen developed a serious drinking problem that eventually led to the breakup of the marriage. When she was 48 years old, Jeannette met and married Mark H. Adams, a prominent lawyer in Wichita, Kansas. She lived the remainder of her life in Wichita. She loved her children and grandchildren and travelled the world. She enjoyed playing poker and bingo. She often spoke fondly of her childhood and of that wonderful time when the country was still new. She died at the age of 92.

APPENDIX

Early Day Customs

By Mrs. James B. Cullison

In relating incidents relative to homemaking by pioneers of Oklahoma, if they seem too strongly colored with the personal and ego, it is because my own experiences were typical of those of the majority of early settlers.

Necessity usually forces us to adjust ourselves to existing circumstances. If one was fortunate to have a one room house boarded up and down and stripped, having a floor, doors and windows, but unplastered, he was considered as very fortunate compared with his neighbor who lived in a tent on a dirt floor with aged parents, children and little babies gathered around a fire made from buffalo chips or maybe the root of the yucca or soap-weed. Into such homes as these beings were ushered into life, also departed that borne from which no traveler returns. Patience, determination and endurance were strong characteristics.

As one saying goes…

"They gathered chips to make their fires, they gathered bones to keep from starving, they gathered their courage to keep from leaving."

Many depended for means to purchase their daily bread almost solely on the sale of buffalo bones to the sugar refineries. Almost without exception they came to this untried land with very little money and practically no household goods. The run on settlement having occurred in the autumn, September 16th, they could plant no crops or gardens till the next spring. They faced a long wait and a winter season with meager means for subsistence or protection from the cold. Homemade chairs, table and beds, constructed chiefly from lumber obtained from boxes was the furniture of the majority of houses. Such plebian foods as salt, pork, dried apples, and rice were considered luxuries by the majority.

The daily diet of many was sorghum, molasses, bread and sometimes coffee. I knew one family who saved a little popcorn, the only thing they could give their children on Christmas, being popcorn balls. When they went to get it, the mice had eaten it, a real tragedy.

It is not to be presumed because these pioneers were subjected to so many hardships that they were unrefined natures. We knew personally two young people, both college graduates, living in a dugout. There came a terrible electrical storm and severe hurricane in the night. Their supply of coal oil had become exhausted. During the storm and in the dark their first baby was born. How they braved the terrors of that night is difficult to conceive.

We ask ourselves the questions, "Why did they face all these difficulties of their own volition." The answer is they must have been actuated by the same spirit which impelled our ancestors to seek the shores of a new land.

With the coming of spring the settlers began to break the sod and plant the few acres they were able to prepare to corn, kaffir, and similar grains, melons and garden. The year was a dry year, then as now gardens did not grow very readily. With "hope which springs eternal in the human breast" they watched the stunted growth in their fields and visioned the growing fields of wheat which they were sow on the ground which had been prepared in the spring.

If they had no other meat, a rabbit supplied the deficiency. A very nice sauce or pie could be made of pie melon providing five cents worth of tartaric acid and a little sugar could be afforded to add tone to the mixture. If pumpkins had been raised in the fall, stewed pumpkin seasoned with spices and molasses was a very palatable dish. If they had no cow to furnish milk, excellent biscuit could be made from sour yeast dough with soda to sweeten. Occasionally, friends back home sent castoff clothing which could be made over, very presentably, by skillful fingers.

Children wore panties then, mothers would bleach flour sacks out of which to make the panties and sit up nights to crochet a little edge for them. Crazy patch dresses. There was always a spirit of comradery and mutual helpfulness. Someway they struggled through the first two years. More rains came the third year bringing better crops and more comfortable living. I do not recall that they ever asked or received aid from the state or government, excepting, possibly seed wheat. When they did not have what they needed they went without.

The spiritual side was not neglected, religious services being held almost from the first day of settlement. Schools were organized within a year and the order of the older communities began to be established. To those buoyant and valiant souls, whose hair is now whitened, some have gone to the great beyond all honor is due. To have had even a minor part in building this great state of Oklahoma has been a privilege. We almost feel we came into the Kingdom for such a time as this.

To Justice James B. Cullison for his Seventy-Fifth Birthday

I used to watch the gray-haired judge each evening after tea, working among his flowers and shrubs, or straightening a crooked tree. I though it strange this learned judge should work with spade and hoe, soil his hands in soft black dirt, to plant flowers row on row. The years wore on, he worked and delved, plucked out the choking weed. Tended the tiny sapling elm, he'd murmured from a seed. I saw the sapling grow, expand into a lofty tree. From summer's heat and winter's blasts, it often sheltered me.

A haven for the feathered-fold, for squirrels and green tree-toads, man and beast within its shade rested from weary loads.

I saw the flowers year after year, flourish, bud, and bloom. And flaunt their colors in the sun and scatter sweet perfume.

And now I know his garden is a symbol for his life, the beauty, peace, and happiness brought to this world of strife.

The evil, calumny, deceit, the avarice, and greed, he banished from the lives of men as he had plucked the weed.

Crooked, bent and broken lives, he mended tenderly, and led them in a straightened path as he had shaped the tree.

A kindly word, a heartening smile to cheer the darkened hour, were scattered freely o the way.

As perfume from a flower.

Three quarters of a century and this is your birthday, would I might gather all the flowers into one huge bouquet. The flowers you've scattered down life's path with happiness and replete and tie them with bands of love and lay them at your feet.

Your daughter,
Irene Cullison Vaught
September 21, 1932

Original Family Poems

The Pioneers

Some years ago, to score I ween behold a land both rich and green, O'er which
the summer's scorching heat, the winter's hail and snow and sleet,

The autumn's lazy, hazy air,
The breath of springtime sweet and rare
With adorous blossom richly laden, whose perfume from some distant Eden
Fell not on schoolhouse, Kirk or Manse, for over all that broad expanse

Of boundless soundless solitude, the Indian's hut, the cowboy's rude
Log Cabin and the railroad station were sole signs of habitation
Save lines of steel which side by side wound in and out, cross country wide

In canyon deep or woodland shade the warrior woo'ed his dusky maid
Told o'er and o'er whose tales and legends of former days and other regions
Nor dreamed he that the time was near when prairie vale and forest dear
Would for a mightier stronger race become a sweet abiding place

But should you search historic lore you'll find all nations fell before
The onward march of Anglo-Saxon from Cedric down to Andrew Jackson
And so we've heard there came a time often told in prose and told in rhyme,
When from north, south, east and west Hordes came on horseback, four abreast
Some came in wagons, some afoot, and some on railroad trains to boot
They captured everything in sight, long ere the day waned into night
Fate's wand brought forth from scenes so tragic, cities and towns, as if by
magic

The wonderous cycles of the years, transformed the homes of pioneers
To stately structures, strong and grand, as grace the face of any land
The fruitful soil her vintage yields, and wave on wave the golden fields
In shimmering splendor rise and fall, like morning light on castle wall

Oh Oklahoma! Unto you we pledge allegiance strong and true.
Adopted land, our love and pride, truth, justice, honor be your guide.

By Mrs. J.B. Cullison

My Baby Boy

Where is my little baby boy

Whose dimpled hands and flower-like face

Once filled my heart and soul with joy, I held him close against my breast

While rocking, rocking to and fro

I soothed him oft' times to rest

Who's this I see on prancing steed

With hat awry and cheeks aglow?

A bonnie lad he is indeed

Why it's my baby boy, I crow!

Each day someone comes blustering in, at evening after school is done

With many a shout and deafening din

And sparkling eyes so full of fun!

Would you believe that it can be

This sturdy lad so strong and gay?

Is this the sweet babe who clung to me?

The one I rocked but yesterday!

Swift flow the years on silent wing

My baby boy, a man is he.

No more to him I'll sit and sing

He'll nevermore come back to me

'Tis eventide and ends the day

My little grandson on my knee

I rock and croon the same old way

My baby boys come back to me.

(Written by Mrs. James B. Cullison about her grandson, Russell S. Cullison)

"Regret"

When I was little and life's road was new,

I sometimes thought if I could choose my way,

The path that seemed all roses fraught with dew and canopied with rainbow colors

gay,

Unto my childish feet would never weary grow, beneath my steps I crushed the

sweetest flowers,

Nor paused to see their beauty, how was one to know.

When longest days seemed but the shortest hours.

That spring but lingered till the building time was o'er

Too soon would follow summers, fruit and flower

And autumn's full fruition come once more

Then winter holds me in its gloomy power

And so I plucked me from the blossoms fair

The transient poppy and the gorgeous rose

And to the wind I flung their fragrance rare, nor garnered aught to cheer me at life's

close

Ah, me! If I once more by chance might tread, the paths that from the present

backward trend

Each wayside flower and bird-song overhead, its sweetness to my wayward heart must

lend.

I'd feed my soul with perfume from above, Frankincense to my heart those things

would be

Unstinted would I revel in God's love, H is each creation would a lesson be to me.

Then from my richness, unto others I would yield though crushed and broken, pained

and sore.

Like flowers, I had crushed, within life's field I'd scatter fragrance all the more.

By Mrs. J.B. Cullison

Dreamers

When the soft silence of the night,

Enwraps me in its gentle fold,

My wandering fancy then takes flight,

I dream sweet dreams of thoughts untold.

When morning gilds the eastern sky,

Her banners to the Heavens unfurled,

Uplifted is my soul, I cry,

In dreams I see a better would

When noontide's fructifying beam

Sheds radiance on lake and field

Exultantly I dream and dream

Of golden harvest's bounteous yield

When soothing twilight shadows fall

My chastened spirit seems to see

And dream and know there's good in all

Life-life you have been sweet to me.

By Mrs. James B. Cullison

"Jeanneane"

Dear little girl with nut-brown hair, smiling brown eyes and coquettish air;

Beautiful hands so dimpled and sweet;

Where will they lead you – those precious feet?

Down pleasant paths be sprinkled with flowers, happy with laughter and bright golden hours;

Or up the bare mountain, rugged and steep? Perchance in the valley's shadowy deep.

Whatever you lot, we breathe a fond prayer, the Shepherd will watch and keep you in his care.

By May M. Cullison

My Grandma

Say fellows, ain't it nice when grandma comes to visit,

She alluz know just what to bring, she just don't seem to miss it.

Mine can jest do anything, sew and cook, an' how!

And tell me stories, sing me songs at that she's jest a wow!

Why she knows stories, yes she does, that she learned years ago

'Bout the Magic Rug and Hootie, and others she does know

My mother, all her stories they have to be read

And they ain't half so nice as those that are just said

My grandma, she makes things, my ma can't make at all

Such as marble bags and knap sack, and woolen shirts for fall

She makes crumb pie, to take to school, and other things I like and want,

Gee! I wished she lived here and we'd take a little jaunt

She even takes a walk with me and tells me 'bout each bird and tree

And tells me things that daddy did, Gosh! He sure must have been some kid!

I don't know why she knows so much, unless it's cause she had two boys to

bring up of her own, my uncle and my dad,

Of course my mother, she's all right and she won't be so bad,

When she gets to be a grandma and I am like my dad!

By Mrs. Jeannette Adams

"Your Name"

Your name is on the warm lips of the rain

That press all night upon my window pane:

I hear it I the early morning breeze

That sings across the meadow land and plain.

I hear it in the soft voice of the brook

That pulrs along our old familiar nook:

I hear it in the shouting of the sea

Down on the beach road we so often took.

A Name so dear to me.

Upon the copper of the evening sky

The fiery hand of sunset writes it high ,

Inscribes it with a mighty pen of flame

That holds spellbound the heart and mind and eye,

Thy loved hallowed name.

And often in the quiet hours of the night

The long white fingers of the moonlight write

Upon my bedroom wall a name that gleams:

A name so beautiful and silvery white

I hold it in my dreams.

By Russell Cullison, age 19

Douglas Cullison

Mary May Sharp Cullison

"Strip"

"One minute before the start"   Sep. 16th 1893

"Strip"

N.W. cor. Chillocco Reserve   Sept 16th 1893

Garfield County Courthouse circa 1910

Phillips University circa 1910

145

East Enid circa 1910

The Cliff House Hotel, Manitou Springs Colorado

Mary Cullison and her daughters June, Irene, May and Janey

Judge James B. Cullison

Judge James B. Cullison and Mary Cullison

Judge James B. Cullison

Jeannette Cullison Adams

Established in 1893, W. B. Johnston Grain is the largest and oldest independent grain and seed dealer in Oklahoma.

W.B. Johnston

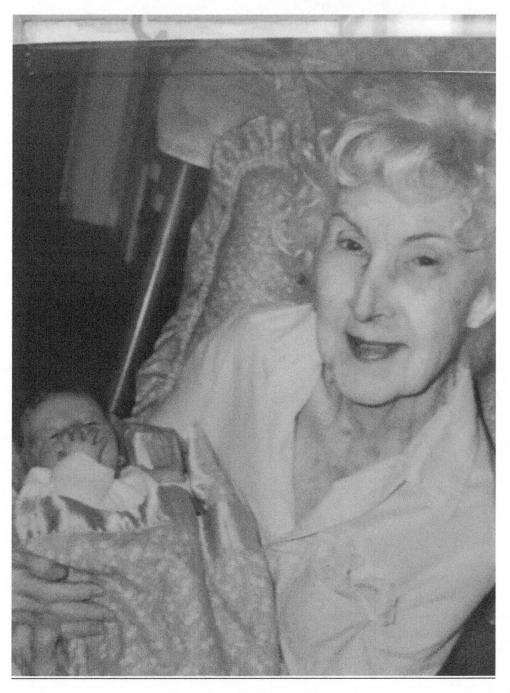

Jeannette Cullison Adams

Glen Johnston

Matilda McCabe – Judge Cullison's Mother

Portrait of Jeannette Cullison Adams

Made in the USA
Monee, IL
06 June 2020